UFOs, Religion, The Origin of Man
Beyond The Controlled Narrative

What They Never Wanted You To Hear

By James Gilliland

UFOs, Religion, The Origin of Man

UFOs, Religion, The Origin of Man: Beyond The Controlled Narrative

Published by James Gilliland

Website: www.eceti.org

ISBN: 978-1-4466-8190-9

From the Beautiful Many Spiritually and Technologically Advanced off Worlders, Ancient Ancestors, and Ascended Masters from all Cultures.

UFOs, Religion, The Origin of Man

Contents

Introduction

This information is about ending the failed 70+ years of disclosure, the Controlled Narrative, and opening Humanity and the Earth to a whole new future. A future that transcends war, disease, poverty, and division. We have the opportunity to join the Beautiful Many Spiritually and Technologically Advanced Off World visitors as part of the Awakening and Healing of Humanity and the Earth, "Ascension". It is our destiny.

UFOs, Religion, The Origin of Man

1. Disclosure 70 Years of Insanity

Most people are starting to wonder with the exponentially increasing sightings around the world, witnesses from every culture, religion and belief why there is so little known about these off world beings. Some are advanced races from Inner Earth who ventured inward during the great floods and did not have to start over as primitives. Others come from the Pleiades, Orion system, Sirius, Lyra, the Andromedin system, a myriad of dimensions yet are seldom mentioned in the controlled narrative. Why are we still focusing on abductions, Roswell, events that happened as far back as 75 years. This includes German back engineering of off world craft since the 30's. Why are we still asking the questions do extraterrestrials and multidimensional beings exist. Why have those who are authentic and have the answers being heavily censored, black balled from the media and the UFO community?

Why are contacts that are happening now like ECETI, ongoing for 40 years with phenomenal photos, videos, eyewitnesses from every walk of life, witnesses like Air Force Base Commanders, Pilots, Air Traffic Controllers, Triple PHD Boeing Engineers, Lockheed Skunk Works Scientists and Engineers being censored? Why when redundantly was the exact location and time of sightings given ahead of time due to telepathic communication, caught on film with multiple eyewitnesses. Why is this being censored. Censored and completely ignored by major Television shows present at the time these events happened like Ancient Aliens and other major UFO documentaries. Why was the incredible footage taken at ECETI sanitized made ambiguous when it was breathtaking? Why has ECETI with again a 40 year history of contact with tens of thousands of eye witnesses been pushed to the side, slandered, attacked at times with deadly force surviving only due to divine intervention? There is only one common sense answer.

"IT IS A CONTROLLED NARRATIVE."

Contact with Spiritually and technologically advanced beings is a threat to the character, the absence of integrity and moral values of those that control the narrative. Before we get into the why's, let's talk about the history and the who's. This is going to get very sticky and some things are going to be said that are going to ruffle some feathers yet this needs to be addressed if we are ever going to have contact with Spiritually and Technologically Advanced off world beings, our Ancient Ancestors, and Advanced Inner Earth Societies.

Humanity is at a point in evolution where they are waking up to the fact that not everything they have been told about God, the origins of man, and history is true. In fact most of it is social engineering that has been going on for a very, very long time. At least 450,000 years when the first known recorded colonies came to Earth from ancient Lyra. They were the great stone workers and temple builders. Some call them Anunnaki or gods along with their offspring the demigods, the rulers of humanity. There were ancient colonies built by the Aheians 600 millions years ago along with the Andromedans unrecorded before the Lyrans, the Nazca Lines are the remnants of the Andromedan society. They had to leave due to something in the Earth frequency that was not sympathetic with theirs. Many became sick.

The ancient Lyrans settled in Australia, then moved to Africa. Humanity did not start in Africa as you are told by archeologists. Many of the first colonies are underwater or ice and they shall remain unknown until the old professors and religious scholars die along with their books based on recycled ignorance. The known beginnings with the oldest records available are in Australia. Gosford Glyphs is just one of many sites. They have tried to destroy it, it was earmarked for a bombing exercise, they carved fake hieroglyphs over the ancient ones, all in an attempt to erase the true history of Earth. The breast plates of the Egyptian Kings came from Australia where the oldest gold mines are found. The reason many of our ancient ancestors were affectionately known as, "cone heads" was because they were the ones with the elongated skulls.

The ancient Lyrans were the giants, the bearded Gods, the temple builders, some over 24 feet tall. Some of the Egyptian rulers known as demigods were their offspring, they were hybrids half human half Lyran. There was cradle boarding where they wrapped the children with cloth and boards to shape their heads to look like the ancient gods yet the ancients with the elongated skulls existed long before this practice. The anatomy of their skulls is entirely different.

Before we continue, we are not diminishing Gods existence. We are going beyond the limited images of the bearded Gods of old. There is the Creator God, the one consciousness that encompasses all consciousness on all planes and dimensions throughout the Multiverse and there are the little g gods, the bearded gods recorded throughout history in the various religions. These beings were ancient, they were very spiritually and technologically advanced yet throughout time some fell and became self-serving. There were turf wars between the ruling families, actions outside of Universal Law. There was a lot of genetic tinkering in those times which is where the half man half animal legends came from. There was a primitive man developing naturally on Earth which was genetically upgraded for various purposes.

One was to serve the Anunnaki which translates to those who came from heaven to Earth or from the skies. The other was a gift to create a quantum leap in evolution depending on the nature of the one doing the genetic engineering and their agenda. A good example is Noah. When he was born he glowed, had white hair and the village did not know what to do. They brought the child to Enki who had an affair with one of the village women. He said that the child is a gift to the village. He will lead you in the days to come. Was this good or bad, it all depends on one's perspective? This is just one story of the creation of demigods. The Greek history is replete with them. For the record Enki was the god that loved humanity, stood up for humanity at the councils. Enlil was a general who wanted the experiment to end and humanity to be wiped off the planet. There is a lot of controversy and claims about these Anunnaki reincarnating through various individuals. It is wise to not follow anyone. Time better spent is making your own personal connection with the one God.

Most cannot believe this same genetic tinkering is going on today in deep underground facilities again for various reasons not as benign. One of them is to genetically enhance super soldiers. Imagine the strength of a tiger and the night vision of an owl. Some of your cryptos come from these labs such as Dog Man, Chupacabra and a few other creatures you don't want to come across in the forests. For the record Big Foot does not fit into this category. They are part of the human experience that evolved in nature, worked in harmony with their environment rather than conquering it. There are different genotypes of Big Foot. More on this later.

In the ancient past there were hideous experiments with half animal half man, the merging of animal DNA with humans. In the past the Minotaur, half bull half human, the Centaur half horse half human, the Satyr or Faun half man half goat. There was also a half crocodile half man which is a genetic engineering feat that to this day cannot be duplicated. These experiments very well may be where the mermaid legend originated. Many could not breed to create offspring so there was no continuance of their species. This is all documented in ancient history, the bones have been found but dismissed as myth by archeologists and universities to maintain the status quo.

In deep underground bases these experiments are ongoing, it is a very cruel adventure. When these being cross over and most live a very short life they are confused. They don't know where to go, are they human or animal? It is making a mess in the ethers. They are stuck trying to get peoples attention. This is the origin of the goat man legend. He appears in peoples dream states often pressing them down. It is a call for help.

There are the positive genetic upgrades to assist in the awakening and healing of humanity and the Earth. Advanced civilizations have added their DNA to the existing human DNA and incarnated to assist in the planetary liberation. Other advanced souls are incarnating which are upgrading the DNA in the bodies in which they incarnate. There is a bit of a war between the soul and the cellular memory or genetics that do not resonate with the higher frequency soul. Some are aware of this, it is what is referred to as star seeds, many are not aware yet but will be activated in the future. The seed is the transfer of DNA from the stars. There are always two sides to the story and it depends on your reference point how you embrace this knowledge.

2. Gods and Goddesses, Ending the Confusion of Religions

The stories of the Gods and Goddesses of old and demigods are not myths. There were the Hebrew Gods, yes there were two. Jehovah, the Hebrews called Jehovah the terrible, the jealous wrathful, what some call the genocidal god of the Old Testament and the New Testament god YHWH, Yahweh the God of love and peace. Many will say it is the same God it is not. The new covenant Jesus or Y'shua, "Y'shua bin Joseph" as he was known by his family brought the new image of God, the all loving, all forgiving God. This understanding is imperative for all Christians who are caught between the two images.

You cannot fear God and love God at the same time. You cannot become one with God if fear is present because in its most unlimited understanding God is pure unconditional love, joy and bliss the highest consciousness and energy. It transcends ego which is why Jesus said I do not judge thee nor does my father judge thee go and sin no more. Sin is actually and archery term. If you sinned, you missed the mark or the target.

Believe it or not there are do-overs, gain the wisdom from the experience, forgive yourself and others and try again. The True Creator is without and ego, without and ego you cannot judge. You will never be punished for merging or becoming one with God and rising or ascending up the vibrational continuum until oneness is achieved. Fear, Guilt and Unworthiness are the tools of the enslavers. Karma is better understood as action/reaction. Although God does not judge or punish, there is karmic law and the relatives or society that does judge and punish. This is why it is best to stay within Universal Law and be kind and loving if you are on the path to enlightenment or ascension.

Contemplate why Jesus said Ye are Gods, children of the Most High. Why his prayer was, "Beloved father let them become one as we are one." Why did he say Ye will do greater works than I for I go on to the Father. How could Jesus say I AM God and pray to God? The prayer was asking Yahweh for assistance in his own walk on Earth to help him maintain his 7th dimensional connection. His ascension process back into oneness, once achieved he was God. Sit with this for a while. It answers the unanswered question for eons, how could Jesus say he was the Son of God and later say he was God and who did he pray too?

This needs repeating in a different way. Jesus's message was his life. He identified as a child as the son of man, the son of Joseph and Mary, Later, he said I am a messenger of God because he was receiving messages from within and delivered those messages in the temples. He then said I am the son of God realizing he was not just a body or a personality, he was a soul born of God. His last message was I AM God. Total at-one-ment, he merged in consciousness with the one consciousness that encompasses all consciousness on all planes and dimensions throughout the multiverse. He was the way shower, the exemplar Christ which is a level of consciousness. He transcended all cultural and religious boundaries and recognized the Creator within all Creation including himself by going within. The temple has always been within because there lies the spark waiting to be ignited into the full flame.

Just speaking about spirituality, the Creator God, or the bearded gods of old is tabu in the UFO community. Without spiritual knowledge, true historical knowledge, we are left with the images and stories of old disconnected from the higher dimensions. There were the Greek Gods/Goddesses, the Hindu Gods/Goddesses, the Asian Gods/Goddesses, the Egyptian Gods/Goddesses, Gods and Goddesses of every culture all existed throughout time. Many still exist to this day, most not in this dimension.

The vehicles of the Gods are replete throughout ancient text. Without this factored in ufology is very weak in its understanding of ancient aliens or ancestors. The benevolent ones are all working together for the betterment of humanity and the Earth. This flies in the face of those who want to keep us divided. The images of the bearded gods and their vehicles, sky ships, came from our ancient past which has been suppressed by governments, religions and universities to maintain the status quo. One who is awakened to their true history, their heritage and divinity is one that cannot be controlled.

This is a most blasphemous truth to those who want the controlled narrative to continue and their worst nightmare. It destroys the controlled narrative and ends the enslavement of humanity through ignorance. The last thing they want is for you to become enlightened uncontrollable and make your own personal God connection. Each religion wants you to be lie ve theirs is the only way and anything outside of their narrative is ungodly. What is ungodly is the divisionary tactics and the wars that often followed. There are no divisions in a God that is omnipresent. Anything that does not fit into religious narratives is shunned and condemned in the past at times with deadly consequences. This is one piece of the controlled narrative.

The false narratives in archeology and history are another. The real history of Earth goes far beyond biblical, historical and most religious understandings. What is taught as history and archeology in most universities is false. Archeologists are constantly rolling back the origin of man/woman. There were advanced humans walking the Earth for millions of years, some of their temples still stand, others are buried under ice, sand, covered by thousands of feet of water while the most ancient are being recycled as molten rock. The plates are always moving beneath one another in a very long recycling process. There are beautiful tunnels smooth as glass have been uncovered 300 million years old. Pyramids are found world wide and they are all connected with these tunnels. You are not going to hear about that in your churches or colleges.

They say the truth will never come forward until the old professors die. Many have written books that are based on the recycled ignorance of the past, anything new will never come forward on their watch. Despite too numerous to mention artifacts found that destroy their narrative. The same goes with religious scholars, heaven forbid their research does not align with the narrative of their religions. One of their biggest problems is everything we are talking about is written into the sacred books of many religions, yet it is either misinterpreted, dismissed or censored. There are golden threads of wisdom that connect all the religions if you look for them. Being kind, loving, respectful, grateful and of service are just a few.

You cannot capsulize God in a book which is what drives many a priest mad. This is why Jesus said, "Ye search the scriptures in vain for I speak of a living God." Nature is your best church, there you can witness the Omnipresent Creator in all Creation. Any questioning mind would ask the question what kind of intelligence designed all this, created the balance, the intricateness, and the vastness. A question you might ask your church is if God is Omnipresent where to I go to find God, why did Jesus say God is closer than the hair on your head? How can God be closer than the hair on your head and not be you? Now before you run off thinking you are the all-powerful lord of others remember God is love and love serves. Narcissism and Spiritual Ego, disempowering people to worship a man/woman or God outside of self is a distraction. Many are trying to establish their own self-worth by creating followers. If enough people love, accept and approve of them they can love, accept and approve of themselves. Humility and service to others is a much more advantageous path.

UFOs, Religion, The Origin of Man

3. Ancient Technology

There are accounts of very advanced civilizations, extreme technology, weapons of mass destruction used in ancient wars resembling beam weapons and nuclear wars. Aero ships with weapons resembling rockets that were heat and sound sensing. Much of the technology is used in your current secret space programs such as mercury drives. When excavating the earth to the time of these recorded events in India where weapons were used by the gods that destroyed forests, tore the skin off elephants, created immense destruction the ground is still radioactive.

The Dead Sea is a byproduct of an ancient very advanced, artistic island civilization that would not embrace Jehovah as their God. It was laid to waste. The glass sheets under the Gobi Desert in the East are the remnants of beam weapons used on Lemurians by the Atlanteans. Atlantis and Lemuria were colonies established by the Pleiadeans which became divided. Their ancestors were from ancient Lyra yet do to adjusting to life on other planets their size diminished. In the past Atlantis worshiped knowledge and science then began to use that knowledge to create technology to control and suppress in some cases destroy their opposition. The Lemurians worshipped the Creator in all Creation and helped those less fortunate to reach their highest potential. They were a threat to the controllers of Atlantis because they were a reflection of their failure to live according to Universal Law. This same scenario is playing out to this day. The tyrants and controllers, verses the lovers of freedom that honor and live under Universal Law most of which is written into the American Constitution and the Bill of Rights. This is why America must never fall it is the last bastion of freedom and imperfect as it may be the foundation is there.

Governments also have played a big role in controlling the narrative. Many governments are controlled by the religious factions within their countries and vise versa. Governments and religions want the status quo to continue, they want people to look to them to tell them how to think, what to be lie ve, what to do. Critical thinking is forbidden. There is the Satanic/Luciferian global network some call the Illuminati or Global Elite, an arm of which is the deep state. It is a global pedophilia ring involved in some very dark rituals. The child sacrifice, sex trafficking and pedophilia is replete throughout these orders. This is being revealed throughout politics, religions, the music and movie industry as of late.

This includes the corporate sponsored news which suppresses anything concerning these subjects. Have you ever wondered why over 8 million kids go missing every year? Presently the government cannot account for over 8,000 children through their foster care programs. Where do they go? Why are 50 kids at a time shipped to foster care recipients only to disappear? It is no longer hidden. They create satanic half time rituals and dress as demons and devils in the music and movie awards.

Most don't realize what they are watching because they don't understand the symbology. They think it is just entertainment. Most cannot even fathom the ritual abuse, child sacrifice including cannibalism going on behind the scenes. This is something I have been very vocal about and abhor which is why you won't see me any longer on the main stage or in any of the major ufo disclosure movements and films. I will leave the details to other authors covering these matters so as not to be thrown into the conspiracy category. As if I am not already.

The overall goal of the enslavers is to keep you in the lower energy centers, survival, sex and power and keep you out of balance, distracted, and emotionally engaged in the lower levels of consciousness. This game is also replete throughout the business industry with images of bronze beauties you get if you buy the right beer, car, or other products they are selling. The moral degeneration and keeping people from the higher energy centers or higher consciousness and energy is by design. It is how you control the people and often referred to as social engineering. Most of your icons, the people you admire, the most famous unfortunately are all in on it. Including the UFO community which has been hijacked from the top down by wealthy Satanic/Luciferian influences, those with the big money. There are the morally and integrity challenged individuals that do their bidding. Some willingly and some in ignorance. The lust for fame and fortune over-rule impeccable integrity, truth and service to the awakening and healing of humanity and the Earth.

"They are the antithesis of contact with spiritually and technologically advanced off worlders, Inner Earth and the ongoing planetary liberation." Although they promise contact they have not risen to the occasion and met the requirements. Many of the conferences now are nothing more that carnivals, reptilian feeding grounds, replete with people lacking in moral integrity trying to sell you something perpetuating the controlled narrative. There are many stories yet where is the evidence? We have the witnesses, the photos, the videos of craft and their occupants. Those who are not authentic are propelled to the top by design.

Somewhere along the line they sold out. Why else would they ignore the mountain of evidence of ongoing contact for over 37 years at Eceti, ignored contact at other spiritual centers, the testimonies of top scientists, Air Force base commanders, pilots, air traffic controllers, people from all walks of life who have witnessed the ongoing contact at Eceti. This includes Elders of all nations.

UFOs, Religion, The Origin of Man

4. Rising to the Occasion

We have to rise to the occasion, not devolve into lessor integrity and decadence seeking fame and fortune, perpetuating the deception and the controlled narrative. We have to do our own research, use critical thinking, look at the history and agenda of each speaker, their true motives. Most are starved for attention lust for fame and wealth and will do anything to stay on top with some of the most ridiculous stories. Others are part of the Rockefeller Initiative, CIA or military intelligence.

One must transcend the controlled narrative, social engineering, and religious programing to make contact with Spiritually and Technologically Advanced off world and higher dimensional beings. Beings which are the greatest threat to the controllers because they know the true history of Earth and the true nature of God. Love, service to others, making one's own personal God connection and knowledge of your ancient past, godlike ancestors is contrary to their agenda. God forbid you come to realize you have the DNA of the gods and God is within you. The original name of Yahweh, YOD HE VAV HE is written into your DNA and is in the process of being activated.

It takes an open mind, pure intent, and a loving heart to make contact with Spiritually and technologically advanced beings without any hidden agendas along with the desire to serve in the awakening and healing of humanity and the Earth. Who in your government institutions, religious institutions, business institutions, educational institutions, the UFO community have met that criteria?

The United Nations has also been corrupted as most of your agencies so don't look there for some ambassador that is going to do anything other than continue with the controlled narrative.

"Now you know why we don't have contact other than a very few, most unrecognized or acknowledged in today's socially engineered society. Especially in the UFO community where the authentic are brutally attacked and censored by the shills and posers."

5. This is One of the Greatest Stories Never Told

This again ties religion to higher dimensional beings. It begins with a question. When Mary was pregnant with Jesus, Joseph said Mary is with child and I have not laid with her, I will not marry her. A being appeared to him, Gabriel as told in the past. He was not of this Earth. He said this is my child or God's child depending on the interpretation and you will rear him as your own. In the strictest of definitions the Father of Jesus was not Joseph, he was non terrestrial. Mary had very pure genetics going back to ancient Lyra. Blending the genetics of Gabriel to her genetics created a superior body.

The soul or life force of Jesus was too strong to reside in a body that was not genetically upgraded. He would have burned out the synapsis. Jesus came from the plane of bliss, the 7th dimension. He was done with the need to physically reincarnate, done with the need of any physical reality. He transcended it or ascended previously. He assimilated the knowledge of 12 Grand Ascended Masters before he incarnated.

He was the thirteenth, the representative of Yahweh the God of love and peace. Each of his disciples represented the nature of each Grand Master.

The sacrifice Jesus made was to leave the plane of bliss and come to Earth to deliver the new covenant, to free the people from tyranny and the image of the wrathful god used to this day to control the people. His life and his message was not a message of subservience it was empowering. He desired that every man/woman make their own personal connection with God. Yahweh was his tether residing in the 7th dimension or the plane of bliss who was supporting him and working through him. The plane of Bliss is a plane of Golden Light, Consciousness and Energy so loving, joyous and blissful there are no words that can fully describe it.

As stated that temple is within. Again it is the spark that has the potential to become the full flame, the one consciousness that encompasses all consciousness in ever expanding states of awareness. It is the true nature of humanity buried under layers of wounds, traumas and wrong conclusions from past experiences, generations of recycled ignorance and social engineering. You might want to read this one again.

How does this tie into UFOs. The Andromedins mythically known as Archangels with magnetized light bodies, eight to ten feet tall with beautiful light ships contributed to the DNA of Jesus on his father's side. The DNA unaltered from ancient Lyra, some of the first colonies was Mother Mary's gift. Therefore, Jesus was an extraterrestrial. His DNA was from Andromeda and the first Lyran colonies. His soul was from the 7th dimension.

There are those of mixed DNA from the stars along with an Earth human that were evolving naturally on Earth. A history the controllers and tyrants do not want you to know. If we can transfer DNA with a laser and turn a frog into a salamander imagine what these extremely technologically advanced beings can do? It is child's play to upgrade humanity. Welcome to my world of blasphemy where true knowledge, real science and enlightenment reigns supreme. Let's see how long you can stay.

6. The Most Ancient Known Civilizations

The most ancient civilizations did not begin on Earth, they began in the stars. The earliest known to humanity is ancient Lyra. The Lyrans were space faring and colonized many systems. They colonized the Orion system, the Pleiades, and the Hyades system before traveling to Earth, Mars and Maldek or to some cultures referred to as Milona. Due to great wars it is now the asteroid belt. These wars also affected Mars which was once a beautiful inhabited planet with lakes, canals and temples. The survivors of this catastrophe went underground, some made it to Earth and both exist to this day along with other colonies. Yes, Earth humans as well now live on Mars colonies.

There were other races throughout the galaxies yet these groups are the most prevalent concerning Earths history. One of the problems with the ancient Lyrans is they always became divided into separate factions eventually going to war. These wars were fought with weapons far beyond anything conventional. This resulted in destroying their home world. That same problem passed to other generations, other colonies. Some transcended it and continued to evolve, others had to start over as primitives due to almost total destruction of their civilizations. This is replete within Earth's history. Due to great wars, natural disasters like mega tsunamis and volcanic eruptions as well as pole shifts humanity had to start over in most cases as primitives. Shut down the grid for a few months and imagine the consequences. Its eventually back to bows, arrows, swords and spears when the ammo runs out. There were lesser evolved souls incarnating from lower levels in the 4th dimension which also added to the devolution of Earth. These are mentioned in the Emerald Tablets which added to the fall.

On the degenerate side of those who came from the stars are Royal reptilians, Dracos, tall Greys, Zetas a smaller version of the Greys. Smaller Greys are in some cases biological robots carrying out the wishes of whoever is in control of them. This is a real grey area, many off worlders are not beneficial to humanity and the Earth and have their own self-serving agendas. There are also insectoids, evolved insects most of which best to avoid.

The Mantis beings have a mixed reputation. The reason for most of the abductions is we have the genes of the Gods. They are creating hybrids to advance their own races. They know how to activate the dormant genes, ones we incorrectly call junk DNA. We have genes for telepathy, direct knowing, the ability to see forward and backward in time, the ability to jump time and space or bilocate as some masters have demonstrated in the past.

Dormant within us is the ability to levitate and activate the salamander gene that allows us to heal, regrow a limb if necessary. We also have the immortal gene. These have all been suppressed in the past yet now they are being activated. Some like many of the Greys are trying to reintroduce emotions into their race. They cannot evolve further and are a dying race because without emotions they cannot make the upcoming shift. Other ETs have strayed so far away from Universal Law their own karma is blocking their evolution. They know the shift is coming and without a major change they will be left behind.

These DNA activations are coming from different sources. Some are due to the changes with the Sun and the addition of a new Sun occasionally visible to the naked eye or caught on cameras which pick up more of the electromagnetic light spectrum. We are entering a highly charged place in the universe. Solar flares, "CMEs" coronal mass ejections, the Schuman Resonance going off the chart, changes in the electromagnetic light spectrum and incoming waves of energy from what the scientists call, "unknown sources."

These activations can also come from contact with those who have Ascended, Spiritually and Technologically Advanced off world visitors. Our ancient ancestors. You cannot engage higher consciousness and energy without a change occurring in your own energy fields. It is called sympathetic resonance; energies seek a balance between the two. Our solar system, our galaxy, our entire universe is evolving, raising in frequency. Those who are not frequency specific no matter what race or culture on and off planet will not make this shift. In other words, the days of tyranny and acting outside of Universal Law are coming to a close. It is time to choose. If you serve the beast you will follow its downward spiral and inevitable collapse. This includes perpetuating the controlled narrative, it is imploding and those who participate in it will be revealed and suffer the karmic consequences.

There are beings too numerous to mention engaging Earth which is why Self Mastery, developing one's own inner sensitivity and learning to set boundaries is imperative. It is not only off worlders and lower dimensional beings with hidden agendas we need to be aware of. Unfortunately, much of humanity on Earth have been preying on their own people. Some under the influence of unseen negative influences, others working out their own karma in ignorance or willingly going against Universal Law. There are many self-serving people wearing the mask of healers, teachers, planetary liberators contrary to their actions. There is a war between the posers, the self-serving and the authentic, those in service to others, those aligned with the awakening and healing or planetary liberation. The deception, greed and corruption are epidemic the depths of which will shock you as it comes to the surface. It shall all be made known and no rock will be left unturned in the days to come.

7. Tell All, Why Contact Can't Happen and Challenges Within the UFO Community

I wish to begin by stating I struggled with writing this next chapter. I struggled with whether or not to release it. The main goal is to bring an understanding to those entering the field of ufology and remove the obstacles to contact. The field of Ufology is not what it seems. Sunshine is always the best medicine. It will also explain why Spiritually and Technologically advanced beings will not participate in these events other than with a very few in the UFO community though many boast contact.

The question we need to ask is with what? It is also an opportunity for those who have strayed off course to get back on track. I am hoping some good comes from this message and a house cleaning begins. I do not expect any of the people mentioned to change, rise to the occasion, and move back into service. They have had every opportunity and time to do so. I do expect the continued censorship and character assassinations that come with being authentic. Let us begin with my entrance into the UFO community.

I was invited to speak at the International UFO Congress by Bob Brown. He seemed to be genuine had a beautiful wife and family, yet I was hesitant. I had written the books, Reunion with Source, Becoming Gods, and the Ultimate Soul Journey. He had read them and asked me to speak at the conference. I told him I was a minister, counselor and more involved with process-oriented therapy, empowering the individual to heal and make their own personal connection with Source. Knowledge of Ascended Masters and spiritually and technologically advanced beings as well as contact comes with the path to enlightenment but in no way do I see myself as an authority. He said I read your books and you seem to be one of the highest authorities.

I agreed to speak and found myself on a 17 hour drive bound for Laughlin Nevada. They still have my presentations from late 90s and early 2000s. The talks were about the spiritually and technologically advanced off world beings and how we need to rise to the occasion. I showed photos and videos of the craft, paranormal manifestations and the beings. People were crying in the audience, there were spontaneous healings and I could barely finish my presentation because I was overwhelmed with the love filling the room by my Pleiadean contacts. The talks ended with standing ovations with the largest rush for copies of the presentations.

During my presentation a person in the audience asked, when are the ships going to appear. I said go out to the river, away from the lights at 11 tonight you will see the ships. I asked myself why in the hell did I say that. It just blurted out. Now I am on the line and if the UFOs don't show my head will be on the chopping block. At 11 that night a massive triangular ship flew over the conference with another saucer shaped ship behind it. A very large orange flash of light came from the saucer shaped ship. It was filmed with multiple eyewitnesses. The speaker from Germany that filmed it bragged about how he knew the ships would come and he will have the best presentation at the conference. Even though I saw him setting up his camera just before 11 and he asked if I really believed they would appear. He gave absolutely no credit for my prediction. Donald Ware also tried to discredit the sightings making a complete fool out of himself saying they were birds. It did not go well with those observing the ships and they made it clear there are no triangular birds with clear edges emitting light or circular ones flashing orange light that resemble birds. The ships were mysteriously erased from the German presenter's camera during his presentation. It was a little lesson in humility. One I found very humorous.

Being naïve to the field of ufology I had no idea how much jealousy and competition was present by other presenters along with other malevolent agendas. That is when the attacks began. I did several more presentations until the jealousy and competition along with board members, some card-carrying CFR members, and a few other spiritually challenged nuts and bolts people created an environment that was not healthy to truth or real disclosure. I always wondered why they professed no NWO, "New World Order" yet these card carrying CFR members were on the board. These same people gave presentations on what a wonderful world the global elite had planned for us. I think we are moving through that now with the epidemics, population control, false flags, planned shortages etc. They want us to own nothing, eat fake toxic meat and bugs. Not the heaven on earth I wish to experience.

Bob Brown told me they were not having me back because I did not cover the fueless energy, anti/counter gravity devices I said I would. What is odd is the devices were covered, filmed while in operation and are in my presentation on video in their archives. Despite the fact that my books and the videos for the presentation were mysteriously hijacked from their office where they were keeping them. If I had not made several copies of the videos showing the technology carrying them with me personally it would have never been seen. Unfortunately releasing the information about the technology resulted in death threats to the scientist, his lab being blown up, car being stolen and numerous shady people trying to acquire it with any means necessary. Which also sheds a dark light on the free energy community.

It is also not what it seems. These same devices were entered in the million dollar prize offered by some of the most well known scientists in the field. It was never ponied up after the undeniable demonstration. The scientists car was stolen soon after thinking the devices were in his trunk. It seemed it took about 5 years before The UFO

Congress had me back. New board members and once the truth bombs settled It was time to give it another shot. The same thing happened, standing ovation, spontaneous healings and major run on the dvds of the presentation.

In Arizona with the new International UFO Congress. Again, I showed incredible new footage of the ongoing contacts with off world visitors and their ships delivering the same message on how we need to rise to the occasion. It was a presentation of who is who in the multidimensional world we live in. I also spoke about unseen negative influences that can influence and hijack your mission. Again, the presentation ended with another standing ovation and the biggest run at the store. They were selling the DVDs of my presentation which had the highest demand at the conference. During the talk I was phasing in and out, tall light beings were seen behind me which was caught on film. People in the audience were showing me incredible pictures. I felt the energies and presences and was aware of it, I did not know it would show up on film. Miraculously it was edited out of the presentation although I retained one of the photos where I turned into a blue green light, all you can see is the microphone.

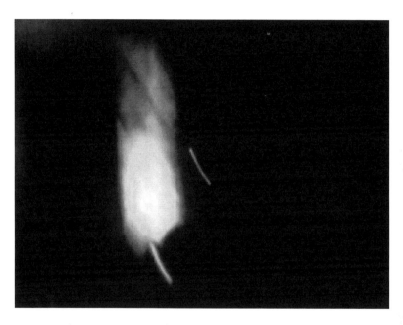

Blue Green Light Phase photo of James

The new owners of the International UFO Congress invited me back saying the people loved you and we are definitely having you back. Later when the next event came around I was met with a very rude Alejandro Rojas after ignoring all my inquiries finally sending me an email saying you are not speaking this year. It seemed the good old boys club met. Again, the controlled narrative rearing its ugly head. As I said before there is a lot of jealousy, competition, back-stabbing, ulterior motives and spiritually challenged people in this field that should not be in any position to decide who speaks and who gets censored. Their claims of being an authority as far as educating people about UFOs are highly overrated with many fitting into the category of nuts and bolts or controlled opposition. These people are why we are still in the dark ages concerning UFOs.

Earlier at these conferences I took the time to share my footage of the beings and ships with prominent people in the field. I handed the video to Richard Hoagland and Steven Greer. Three steps later it was tossed in the trash or on a chair. I was stunned. Nether were interested in contact unless it was through them. It was a real eye opener. I was interviewed for two days for the movie Thrive. Foster Gamble who I still hold as honorable said I gave the most succinct interview with solutions he has heard. I was told I would be keynote in the movie Thrive. Then Greer met with the producer and I was on the cutting room floor. I wonder if the interview still exists, it is as true today as it was years ago.

At Contact in the Desert Greer made some very slanderous remarks about ECETI inferring we are a bunch of hippies on drugs and if you want to make real contact you have to go through him. Quite the enlightened Sanskrit speaking Yogi he professes to be who ironically thinks he is the UFO messiah. The problem is we have a no drug or alcohol policy and I do not do any drugs, plant medicines or drink alcohol. Yes, sounds boring but actually, having a multidimensional mind is not. I would also look into any pujas or meditations to Shani, who according to ancient writings is a demon also known as Lucifer aligned with Saturn. Funny how that keeps popping up, lots of talk about Luciferian or Saturnian death cults lately. Oh wait, didn't Greer publicly say we have to reduce the population? Did the light go on, the bell ring yet? I believe those who want to reduce the population should begin with themselves if they are truly committed.

The two near death experiences I had opened the door and gave access to all the dimensions all the way back to Source. I can see the unseen puppet masters behind the speakers who have agendas and sold their souls for fame and money. I have personally watched Greer give his speech to a scientist with free energy technology saying without me you will never get this technology out followed by I need 51% controlling interest in your device. The next question is where are these devices? He has been given hundreds of thousands of dollars to bring out these devices. He just keeps asking for more money? I am not saying Greer does not have contact, people should be questioning with what. Those who are clairvoyant know. I also question his boasting about ties with the Rockefellers, the Clintons, the Podestas along with where the money actually went from donations and the films. Research the Rockefeller Initiative and see who in Ufology is aligned with them. Then you will have some idea how long and how deep the controlled narrative goes.

During the ECETI Contact Initiation ceremony at Contact in the Desert some very respected investigators in the field of ufology counted over 85 ships. There were more witnessed outside the group with incredible stories. There were orbs and light spheres everywhere again well documented. These same investigators also attended the Greer C-5 initiation where according to them he batted zero other than what he calls a couple anomalous points of light. If you see a plane, hear a plane and notice the strobe and running lights you cannot say it is a plane according to his protocols. You have to say it is an anomalous point of light to rack up the UFO count. There is also the nearby China Lake facility with their experimental craft whistleblowers say consists of anti/counter gravity. Some people did report a few anomalies later on in the night after his event.

Photo of the crowd coming to see James speak at Contact in the Desert

He professes to be able to see ships where no one else can due to his heightened spiritual abilities. Those that actually do have those abilities don't seem to back him up. Others that worship him do see the invisible ships mainly due to peer pressure. I also found it odd that at an Ambassador Training he held at ECETI, our previous staff set up while I was out of the country. A workshop which I was in disagreement of holding, he didn't show up for the first few nights. I ended up holding space until he finally showed up. There was incredible UFO activity before his arrival. He spent the next few days talking about himself which did not go well with the people who spent thousands to be there. It also negatively impacted the Sky Watch. He stated the only reason ships are being seen at ECETI was because of him.

This is a pattern with Greer when going to other UFO hotspots. Problem is there is a long history of ships appearing at ECETI which is at the base of Mt Adams, a well known UFO hotspot. Native Americans, The Yakima Nation has a long history of contact, Kenneth Arnold who coined the word flying saucers witnessed silvery disks descending on the western slopes of Mt Adams. Greg Long,

David Akers and Dr J. Allen Hynek also witnessed the ships. There were also numerous forest rangers and fire tower operators who witnessed the ships long before Greer ever set foot at ECETI which has had 37 years of documented contact. I believe that is long before Greer entered the field of ufology. I won't go into other experiences with Greer, I myself and others witnessed, they are to gross to mention.

The Greer group tried everything to get me to sign an NDA concerning anything that goes on during his event cannot be shared. I declined. This is why others cannot come forward with what they know, and they know a lot. In the interest of transparency lets tear up those NDAs Steven let them tell their stories.

Billy Meier is another interesting character. According to Michael Horn who owns the Billy Meier franchise for the US. The Plejarians as he refers to the Pleiadeans searched the entire planet to find Billy Meier the most enlightened person to be their ambassador. Billy went to prison for theft, joined the Foreign Legion, deserted, became a smuggler, a bounty hunter then wrapped a towel around his head and became a guru. This brings into question the discernment of his contacts. The videos and pictures of his ships did not stand up to scrutiny by top people in the field of CGI, inventors of Adobe editing programs said they were overlays and the film was altered. Finding exact replicas of the ships at his farm along with his wife's testimony which also cast a very dark shadow on his story also did not help his case.

I had his coffee table book with all the ships in it and truly was hoping his contacts were real. Unfortunately, his female contacts bore an exact resemblance to the Dean Martin backup singers. Most likely if he did have contact it was with back engineered German ships, the Dark Fleet or some other lessor evolved beings judging by their behavior. I received many a slanderous email from them along with public defamation of character remarks all because I sent them a copy of the ships filmed at ECETI and later due to their behavior questioned their claims.

The Meier group boasted to be the only ones on Earth having contact and all others were charlatans and frauds viciously attacking the character of researchers, other well documented contactees, ECETI included. They also claimed Billy was chosen by God and claimed to have lofty past lives of known Ascended Masters. They demanded 20 percent of your income to join their group which makes it understandable to claim an exclusive. Michael lost one debate after another yet acted as though he won, a legend in his own mind. I was on a panel with him and dismissed his claims up front as illogical. My question was with the mountain of evidence others are having contact how can you claim to have an exclusive? On the panel I said if someone comes to you and says they are the one stop shopping place for God and ET having an exclusive grab your wallet and run. Then we watched him stumble through his claims. There is no purposeful good in having a discussion or logical debate with him, it's a real crazy maker.

Mufon was another problem, not all groups but some. In the past there was an inside joke. They called Mufon the unpaid agents. Not sure if some on the highest levels were paid alphabet agents, according to rumors allegedly they were. For years they would not address the spiritual side of contact. It had to be nuts and bolts. There was a major scandal having to do with parties with underage women at one MUFON. This is public knowledge. I was invited to go to one of those parties. I declined.

At the International UFO Congress another incident happened. A very young and beautiful woman knocked on my door saying she needed to use the bathroom. I had a bad feeling but could not say no to a woman in need. I immediately called a few friends and asked them to come up right away, I felt I was being set up. With the friends in the room she could not pull off the usual incriminating scam, sex with a minor something many in the field of ufology have been falsely accused to end their careers. I have always been warned ahead of time which has kept me out of a lot of trouble. If they cannot assassinate your character they will throw road blocks censoring your message and as a last ditch effort use deadly force. There was divine intervention a few times avoiding assassination attempts. Bullets whizzing by my head, brake lines being cut, lug nuts taken off the left front wheel to pull you into oncoming traffic.

The Mufon in Seatlle with Peter Davenport who runs UFORC, UFO Reporting center also ran major interference. He was a Russian translator with NSA. He constantly attacked ECETI, denied verifiable reports of UFOs landing in the area. One ship actually picked up an Elk with a lot of trouble getting it on board. It had to circle the area at low elevation with multiple witnesses working for the Forestry Dept. Peter moved locations of sightings, sent engineers to discount the UFO activity only to have them verify the ongoing UFO activity. He then lied about their reports on his network. I cataloged all of it. My Pleiadean contact told me not to engage just document what he is saying.

After massing a mountain of evidence of the deception and bias I was finally told to release it. Blaji, my Pleiadean contact said unfortunately the drama is what gets the message out in today's society. It spread like wildfire opening many doors to tell my story. The lie travels twice around the world before the truth has time to tie its shoes. Sadly, this also concerns gossip and rumors. This time the truth as it always does eventually destroyed the lie along with the character of the one doing the character assassination perpetuating the lies. When you go up against a higher dimensional plan karma is almost instant.

Art depicting Pleiadian Blaji

Snapshot of Pleiadian Ship filmed by James

I had a great time speaking with David Morehouse author of Psychic Warrior. He told me of his encounter with huge golden beings when he tried to remote view the ranch. He went up to my mother and told her, Wanda do you know who your son is, I wish I had the contacts he is having. It was right after she told me I had to dress like him, get a suit and brief case to be acceptable. She was shocked. Robert Dean who gave me some very good advice about the wolves in sheep's clothing. He said never change your story, always speak the truth don't embellish it in any way, they are waiting for you to screw up. We had quite a few long conversations over time and radio interviews. We had a campfire one evening and he said get me a whiskey and a cigar and I will tell you all I know. He made good on that.

John Mac was another. He said he was extremely interested in coming to ECETI and experience the contacts. Unfortunately, he was killed in England by a truck driver just weeks before he was planning to come. I was honored to speak at his eulogy. For those with eyes to see he attended his own eulogy in spirit and was experiencing the other dimensions of which he was researching.

Out of respect for the family I did not mention it though others experienced the same thing.

Jim Mars was one I admired due to his investigative abilities. He did not pull any punches and was on to the corruption in governments and agencies as well as the controlled narrative. He had the opportunity to witness the ships first hand at ECETI. I do not feel his death was of natural causes. He knew too much.

Clifford Mahooti was a real character. We got along very well. He often called out the censorship of Native American cultures where off-worlders have always been a part of their culture. I always looked forward to seeing him and had him speak at the ranch on a couple of occasions. He had an interesting encounter with Big Foot as many others on the ranch. He did the opening prayer for one of our recent conferences with Lakota songs from Jen and Brian. I was on stage with him and I asked who were the two twin brothers with silver shields hovering over the crowd? He smiled, nodded his head and said that was what he prayed for, it is part of our culture, a song for protection.

There were a few others in the international conferences I enjoyed meeting with yet there were so many agendas it made my head spin. Many wanted me to validate their stories, get me on board sadly to say I could not with some. Later their stories turned out to be money making scams or cries for attention. There were many people I supported and launched their careers either at the conferences at ECETI or through the radio show. As You Wish Talk Radio on BBS and ECETI Stargate on Rumble and other channels. Many became opportunists and turned on us as soon as they had the chance. It is the rise to power and fame on the backs of others scenario. Karma is almost instant on that one. Some volunteered, came to the classes and events. They gleaned all the knowledge I shared, we fed and housed them, then they decided they are the true contactees, ambassadors, the chosen ones to lead. ECETI and I had to take a back seat. It was either spiritual ego or the influences of unseen negative influences at play. This usually went on for a while then ended when I mentioned guess who taught you everything and guess who's name is on the deed. This was followed by demands in some cases with threats of extortion. We actually saw some of them shape shift with some pretty scary creatures overshadowing them.

We can usually clear these unseen negative influences but not in the case where someone has locked themselves in, invites them and choses to work with them. Luckily more than one of us saw it, if not we would not have believed our eyes. Just mentioning this will label you as a crackpot, delusional by those without the ability to see beyond the veils. I find it amusing the arrogance of some, those locked into their spiritual egos and physical reality. Sadly, most are too attached to their story and cannot be healed or reached.

Some went public with their stories after being asked to leave that were so ridiculous we did not even comment. I won't go into details it was both sad and ridiculously funny at the same time. They received many warnings, we asked them if they are perfecting their exit strategy with the divisions, disruptions and power struggles. Not one of them took responsibility which is why they were asked to leave. This has continued to this day.

One of the latest incidents is being slandered on social media by radio show hosts after an event in North Carolina where some very serious accusations were made. This all began when I asked the promoter if there were any healers or massage therapists in the group. I have a back injury, one that was so severe the doctors said I would never walk again. I lost all feeling and use of my right leg for almost a year and it is still playing catch up. Deep massage and chiropractors are the only thing that keeps me upright. I work hard on the centers usually sunup to sundown cutting firewood, building, doing repairs, maintenance, gardening, personal counselling, clearing unseen negative influences. All of this takes its toll on the body.

After two planes, two car rides lugging heavy baggage, books and other gear my back was done in. Standing on a stage for 2 hours was something I was not looking forward too. The next thing I knew I was a sexual predator liken to Jeffery Epstein with false accusations and rumors flowing like a river. When asked who was the victim, they could not come up with anyone. I asked who was I unkind to, who did I mentally emotionally or physically abuse, mislead, have sex with? Where was I when this happened, I must have missed it.

The only thing I am guilty of is telling a couple of spiritually incorrect jokes which triggered the person who made the accusations. She really needs to hang out with Lamas and Yogis, the enlightened ones have a wicked sense of humor and are definitely not spiritually PC correct. I am an enigma, well grounded and love humor. I feel laughter is healing, it lightens the load and brings you closer to God. Using spiritually incorrect humor can show people where they have judgements, where the ego needs defending as well as any wounds, traumas or wrong conclusions from past experiences. What we call the big red buttons.

Despite the PC incorrect humor, I can connect to and bring in the highest consciousness and energy due to my NDEs and over 50 years of intense training with Yogis, Lamas and other process oriented therapists. People need to feel comfortable with you before they open up and showing them you are just a normal guy allows this. It is a soft opening of doors to higher consciousness and energy. I have always felt the PC correct agenda was a method of mind control, social engineering at its best and it is epidemic in the woke crowd. It is not uncommon at ECETI to hear that's what she or he said jokes among the staff. If PC incorrect humor is not okay and judgement makes one feel superior we suggest not coming to ECETI.

These rumors at the NC conference were called out and the perpetuators had to admit there was no foundation to their story. The very people the rumors were about called out those making the accusations saying it was all their own projections. Some of these people were married. Imagine this vile gossip getting back to their husbands and family. Rumors can have serious in some cases harmful and deadly effects. In counseling when people ask us if they should leave their husbands or wives we make it very clear we cannot answer that question.

All we need to add to our problems is an angry husband or wife blaming us for their divorce. Unfortunately, others in the field who are very well known, prominent in ufology would say yes, demonize the husband and then hook up with the wife later. Some blaming it on their reptilian parents. Believe it or not reptilian influences are not uncommon in the UFO community. Reptilians, Tall Greys, Serpent Beings, Djinn and other unseen negative influences are often behind a lot of nonsense we have to deal with. There are also wounded people who automatically side with one sex or the other due to their own unhealed past, victim patterns tainting their guidance and counseling sessions.

These rumors and gossip were used by radio show hosts to create division, distance between Eceti and funding what seemed to be an attempt to redirect the funding to them. These are people we highly promoted in the past and helped them advertise their conferences through our network. I told the staff I have already seen where this will go with these two and it will end in betrayal. This was years earlier. It is a classic example of one finger pointing forward with three pointing back when it comes to rumors of sexual predation, one is threatened by and in denial of his own masculinity thinking he will score brownie points in the woke community. He falsely believes playing the role of white knight saving women spreading vile unsubstantiated rumors will elevate his own status.

Actions like these usually stem from childhood trauma, a father that either abandoned them or was abusive. It is not the expression of self-proclaimed enlightenment. Both are opportunists believing they can rise on the backs of others. If they want to pass judgement they don't have to go any further than their own back yard. Their next obvious move as done with others will be to case build to deflect from and validate their morally challenged actions as righteous. In their high opinion of themselves assassinating one's character and stealing their funding is a self-righteous act yet only if they can demonize their target. This fits into the category of narcissism, spiritual ego, being morally and integrity impaired.

I would love to get the names of these victims, they are like ghosts just as the ghosts at the North Carolina event. I would love to question them directly as to when I preyed upon them, lied to them, said one harsh word, abused them emotionally or physically, pressured them in any way. It never has been my nature. Right now these radio show hosts and event coordinators have their own problems due to some they have promoted in their conferences not being who they say they are. Some with a very checkered past from not being truthful to rape and pedophilia. Looks like a little karmic backlash. Maybe a little mirroring there. Take the beam out of your own eye before addressing the splinter in another, a lesson to be learned.

Some encounters I have had with women in the past had affiliations with alphabet agencies, have chips and a family history of working with or tied to these agencies, military intelligence or Milabs. I watched one recently come to visit, have a complete meltdown then became extremely embarrassed by her behavior. It was completely opposite her stage persona. She had to make up a story to distract from what really happened. She said wow, I have met my match as if there was some kind of competition or agenda because I would not participate in her drama. Again, there was absolutely no intimacy other than a hug when she arrived.

I made it clear on several occasions that option was not on the table. She had a splitting headache when she arrived, posted on Facebook how she hates Hawaii informing me immediately she doesn't cook which transferred the responsibility for me to cook, clean and entertain her? I certainly was not raised this way, always thought it was about service, working together. I don't do well with self-importance or entitlement programs. I was on the phone to the staff saying get me out of here, I wanted to leave the Hawaiian paradise some of my staff and I worked so hard to create. She left early due to my refusal to participate in her dramas begging me not to ever talk about what happened. Sadly, she then spread malicious gossip in a first strike attempt avoiding personal responsibility for her behavior joining the other posers threatened by the authentic.

There was also the fact that she could not get what she wanted which was to use myself and the platform of ECETI to further her career. When she asked to visit we set a time when my staff was present to hopefully avoid any drama. When she found out the staff was leaving a couple weeks later, she changed her flight to the day after they left. It was a big red flag for me as to an opportunistic agenda. She is one of the fictitious 8 which has boiled down to two we will talk about later.

This brings us to Manchurian candidates, honey traps, people programmed to derail your mission and keep you in a state of confusion. Yes, this is real and I experienced it on three previous occasions. Totally fell for it once, the second time I was very suspect, the third I saw it coming a mile away. I was naïve going into the UFO community. In my case it was drop dead gorgeous women used to derail the mission. One was a famous super model. I kept asking myself what do these women see in me. I never felt any depth of love then the hammer dropped. Extremely cruel behavior that would tear the heart out of any man. This was by design and I was not the first to succumb to these take downs. Not all sexual predators are men, the me too movement has two sides, covers both genders along with a few other pronouns. Never take sides until you hear both sides of the story and discern from the heart what is true.

I as others have had relationships in the past that didn't work out despite doing everything in my power to make them work. I have never been into multiple partners and have always been honest and loyal to the partner I was with. The truth be known it was never me that betrayed the trust in the past. The ones making those accusations in each case where the ones that betrayed the trust. It is the classic accuse others of what you yourself are doing which seems to be epidemic in today's society. Try as one might some relationships have just run their course and it is not beneficial to either to continue. Even in parting I did everything to make sure it was on good terms and did what I could to insure their well-being. Sometimes that is just impossible. In today's divisionary culture being a seemingly white, heterosexual healthy successful male is a threat to a demoralized and divided society by design. Now days it is an instant guilty verdict for almost everything that goes wrong on the planet. Actually, I am not totally white, my grandmother was Cherokee.

I would love to have a woman at my side, there is nothing I cherish more than the nurturing of the divine feminine. One that could maintain a frequency of love and support as I do that is strong enough to not be influenced by unseen negative influences without any hidden agendas. A woman that would take personal responsibility for her own healing, not project and blame. Especially one with a sense of humor. Unfortunately, that is very rare.

UFOs, Religion, The Origin of Man

8. The History of Relationships

Having full knowledge of advanced civilizations, the love, joy, bliss and freedom in their relationships makes it hard to function on Earth. Women throughout history have not been treated very well on Earth. In the past when you conquered a village you took the gold and the women. You had your way with the women, sometimes selling them or tossing them out for a younger woman. This is still happening to this day to one degree or another, more so in Middle Eastern Countries where the rights of women have diminished, some lower than a pet.

There is cellular memory, past life memory and trauma from this life that creates the insecurities and projections. Males have their issues as well. If you are a male, whether you participated in any of these endeavors, you will be paying for them. Males over the years have had to always be the provider, compete, go to war etc. Those with abusive fathers also have a lot to deal with. When you are in the presence of someone that is vibrating on a higher frequency or living on a vortex or power center this all comes up. Almost immediately in some cases, days, weeks years in others. Imagine standing in the presence of a higher dimensional being with all your wounds, traumas and wrong conclusions from past experiences being amplified and mirrored. Now you know why I spend a lot of time alone, in nature or being creative building or gardening with just a few people at a time. It's a process, we have to take personal responsibility for our emotions and what is surfacing, rise to the occasion.

As a process oriented counselor, I have always supported this process as long as one does not go into blame or projection and one is ready to take personal responsibility and heal. The vibrational lifting, healing and awakening process we are now going through is bringing all this up. Relationships are tough and what many are experiencing is nothing short of end time madness.

9. The Woes of Public Figures

Sadly, when you are a public figure this comes with the territory. There will always be trolls for various reasons. "Haters always Hate." There is a lot of jealousy, competition and projections. People with father issues where you become their father. If you are successful, you are a mirror to their lack of success. There are some that are angry because you are heterosexual, love women and don't desire to be intimate with men. There are some that are just plain nasty people without a life who are unsuccessful, feel unloved, see an opportunity to draw attention to themselves crying out for attention at your expense.

There are those who blame others for what they themselves are doing to deflect any negative attention towards themselves or their actions. Some are opportunistic and believe they can raise their standing in the community on the backs of others. Then there are the narcissists, the shills and controlled opposition. With this mix how can you ever find unity or agreement, maintain a higher level of consciousness necessary to make contact with advanced off-worlders?

The biggest adversaries as of late are the posers. When I realized their story was false and when I refused to validate it in this life as guidance revealed all they had left was to make ridiculous accusations and attack the messenger. People show up at ECETI with claims I am their soul mate, we are married on another dimension, we are telepathically communicating and I invited them to the ranch. There are women, some I have never met talking about wild affairs, quite flattering if it was true, sorry I missed it. This same thing happened to Corey, David Wilcox warned Corey about how women throw themselves at you at conferences and other events. I was a bit naive about that when I entered the field. I have since learned to keep more to myself or with a few close trusted friends.

Believe it or not it gets even crazier. We have had several people claiming to be Jesus some knowing Mother Mary has appeared often at the ranch saying their mom, Mother Mary said I would give them the keys. There are those claiming to be super soldiers, part of the secret space fleet yet it does not add up when they go over their childhood. We have had countless people claiming to be Cleopatras, Mother Mary, Joan of Arcs, etc. sadly their lives now are in total disarray. As I said when people come with agendas and when those agendas are not fulfilled they become victims. It is the classic kill the messenger especially if you don't like the message. I do not begrudge these people they are just looking for love, acceptance and approval externally. In most cases what they did not get as children. Everlasting love acceptance and approval comes from within and you don't need anyone else to mirror it back to you. If people don't reciprocate or acknowledge you, you won't become a victim if you have done your inner work.

Again, anyone who knows me will tell you I am the most unaggressive kind and generous person you will ever meet, ask my present staff. None have signed NDAs. We do all we can to help those who just may not have all their oars in the water. My staff have seen all of this and have been a godsend in handling these challenges. It is and never has been my nature to ever take advantage of anyone in fact it has been quite the opposite. I am usually the one taken advantage of, yet this is my lesson. Because of my nature I have never been good at setting boundaries. I never give up on people hoping everything can return back to basics, being kind and loving.

I have been repeatedly told it is not 25 strikes and then you're out. I do not see myself as a victim, I am learning lessons in trust, setting boundaries and depersonalizing these challenges practicing loving detachment. Confucius says when a person is saying trust trust trust, it's time to count your spoons spoons spoons. One master told me trust is earned don't give it freely. This is a big lesson for a lot of light workers. A Tibetan Lama told me you have had many lives with us, you cannot do cave this lifetime. Your journey is the hardest, mastering basic human relationships. I did not realize the truth and gravity of his words at the time. Now I understand.

This is a very dysfunctional planet. Relationships on Earth are tough. If you resonate on a higher frequency it brings up everything in those around you that has not been healed in their past. It is called sympathetic resonance or not being frequency specific. I have seen in minutes sometimes hours everything come up. The Ranch does that due to the nature of the vortex and its high vibration. Everything of a lower vibration surfaces, wounds, traumas, and wrong conclusions including past life traumas come up. It is an opportunity to heal yet unfortunately most tend to project and blame. I have had projected on me the emotional trauma of every man this life and past life that has every harmed some women, usually in a very short time. It is the same with men who were abused or did not get the love and attention of their fathers. If I was a woman the projection would be what they did not get from their mothers, the female staff members often have to deal with this. Maybe the staff will one day write a book, most would not believe it as to what we have endured.

As in all communities people often join to get what they did not get as a child. Acceptance, love, approval etc. and when you do not give them what they need you become their father, mother even their X lover and the drama begins. As a process-oriented counselor, I understand the amplification and mirror effect often called the wake of a yogi but it's really getting old. I even made a Tshirt that says I am not your father, your mother or your x lover I'm just sitting here.

There are times I just have to say time out, make a list of everything we have done to harm you, embarrass you, any acts that were inappropriate in any way that validates the energies being projected on us. They would come back with an empty piece of paper. Very rarely will you get someone who is going to take personal responsibility. Being a victim is so disempowering, supporting victims is even more disempowering. Saviors need to ask themselves what is the gain they are looking for supporting victims? Does it prop up the ego, do they desire something from the victim? Victims need to ask themselves what is the gain in being a victim, are they getting emotional or financial support by telling their story, locking them into the pattern? Let's be brutally honest. What is the gain in taking personal responsibility? It's called spiritual freedom, taking back your power stepping out of the drama and ascending. Back to the list.

10. Back to the List

Alfred Weber and Jon Kelly also publicly slandered me over an event that never happened. The woman they cited as being involved wrote them a personal email stating clearly I was a perfect gentleman, she was dealing with her own issues surfacing and their story was false. I personally made sure they got it. Alfred Weber posted the slanderous false information on his website. None the less neither issued a retraction. Some of my staff joined in, the Holy Ones only to be totally embarrassed when they read the letter totally exonerating me.

Andrew Basagio who was with Alfred Weber also was screaming accusations about a friend Tanya at ECETI. When they became separated, he began making false accusations screaming in the Sky Watch field he knows I kidnapped her, holding her against her will making threats. Again, Tanya said none of that happened, I was a perfect gentleman. The only thing that did happen was we had a beautiful conversation and I loaned her a car to get back to her hotel when they abandoned her at ECETI. It is a 70 acre ranch, there is a lot going on, not everyone hangs out in the same place with often several events going on. Again, no apology from either.

Richard Boylan a psychologist who lost his license claimed to be the champion of the children, the star seeds. We won't go into how he lost his license. He attended a sweat lodge at ECETI with Golden Light Eagle and other chiefs in the Lakota and Sue nations. People I hold in high regard. Some have crossed over yet in spirit they are not far away. Richard left before the first round of the sweat lodge. He then showed up as a speaker at one of Golden Light Eagles Star Knowledge conferences and started making slanderous claims I was a mason with the illuminati and he had proof. It was like Adam Schiff making claims of Russian collusion having proof against Trump, inside information when there was none. I have no affiliation with any lodge.

There were a few Native American sweat lodges in the past, that is as far as anyone could go with that accusation. This is so ridiculous it hardly bears mentioning. I do not know Boylan's motives for making such outlandish and ridiculous unverifiable claims publicly other than his own embarrassment at the sweat lodge or the reflection of his own lack of authenticity. For a psychologist to act in this way is beyond unprofessional.

The rumors also include running a Russian Bestiality Cult. I have never been to Russia and don't even know what a Russian Bestiality Cult is? Is that sex with bears, farm animals or something? Another incident that comes with being high profile is while in Mexico I did an interview with a gentleman that was one of the producers in the movie Roswell. He owned Fish Taco in Sayulita, Mexico. My brother was with me with his two daughters. We here having a meal before the interview and my niece took a photo of all of us standing in the restaurant which as most Mexican restaurants has a tequila bar. She posted it on Facebook.

Within moments the accusations started, how dare you, those women are half your age, why are you hanging out in bars, you're a hypocrite etc. etc. The wild accusations started flying. I posted the picture with a caption, this is my brother and two nieces . I consumed no alcohol that night, we had dinner before the interview and almost every Mexican restaurant has a bar. Again no apology, no thanks for the clarification. The most salacious statement flying around was I was a convicted pedophile despite years of calling out the pedophilia, child and sex trafficking. One of the main reasons I am blackballed in Hollywood and social media is for addressing these atrocities. Including in the UFO community. A woman found a pedophile in jail with almost the same name only the middle name was different. His middle name was Wilson mine is Alan. Being in jail might have been a clue and seeing me in public at the same time is obvious I was not the same person. I had to post my driver's license to squash that rumor and again no apology, no retraction.

11. Ancient Aliens, Disclosure or Entertainment

Ancient Aliens asked if they could do an episode at ECETI. They came to ECETI with remote viewers John Vivanco and Peter Slattery both completely validated the ongoing contacts giving detailed information we have given earlier. They remote viewed some of the objects flying overhead nailing them as satellites as determined earlier using NASA data. It was made very clear some were not satellites. Some were massive, colorful and responsive to the people on the ground. According to the remote viewers the ships had what they described as Angelic beings on them. They observed the feline beings, the activity within the mountain and the ongoing contacts with many races. I sat with them for over an hour explaining who was on the ships, their agendas, their past interactions with humanity all of which was censored. The only thing you see of me is my hand reaching for a camera.

I called out the producer ahead of time noticing the way he was filming the show. I told him you are going to censor everything concerning me on this show. Please be honest, I am a very busy man, don't waste my time if you are not going to do justice to this story. Of course he said we would never do that. Was it my stance against the child and sex trafficking that got me censored? They post on my sites concerning their tours etc. Almost everyone on the promotional flyer has been to ECETI and knows we have had over 37 years of documented contact far beyond pointing fingers at 3D German back engineering, Roswell, government back engineering. Having their necks cranked back to the past does not allow them to see contact is happening now.

What is it about ongoing contact with Spiritually and Technologically advanced off-worlders that is so threatening? Is it the fact that they have impeccable integrity, high moral standards, operate under Universal Law, have fueless energy, anti/counter gravity, miraculous healing technology. Is it because they have transcended all religious and cultural boundaries, conquered disease and poverty, have their environments in order? As you can see this is what the controlled narrative is keeping from the people. The benevolent Spiritually and Technologically advanced off-worlders are a direct threat to those who wish to keep you ignorant and enslaved through dependency. It has always been my mission to bring all these advanced civilizations have to offer to humanity and the Earth, yet it has been met with extreme prejudice.

UFOs, Religion, The Origin of Man

12. More Backstabbing

Last but not least my X radio show producer was another situation. He was either late or did not post altogether almost every other show. There was always a reason. I was beginning to wonder if he was there for another reason, he was doing a great job of sabotaging the show. It is sad when there is so much adversarial energy from the outside, hacks, trolls and glitches etc. to deal with and then things get sabotaged from the inside.

We spent thousands of dollars on new equipment, there was always something new he needed. He wanted to add commercials take percentages while at the same time speak of being a volunteer, proud to help get out the message. People would ask me if I was going to have a show tonight, I would have to answer not sure. It was a very unstable relationship as it has been with others he has worked with. The final blowout was him disappearing for days with no one able to contact him, there was no show, no way to go live because he had all the passwords then blamed it on us.

Apparently, he was hospitalized for something and went into a victim mode accusing us for not caring for him when all we did was try to find out what happened to him, concerned for his wellbeing wondering whether he was still alive. After over a week he finally contacted us followed by a major meltdown unlike the continuous minor meltdowns then he quit. After all the preceding problems I thought it was best we severed our relationship and did not try as many times in the past to forgive and heal the situation. The forgiveness quota was far exceeded, so was the 3 strike rule. People never knew if the show would air on time or air at all and I could not say one way or the other due to past performances.

He is the major one spreading the malicious gossip about the imaginary 8 women he rescued that were preyed upon. He has given two names, one was the one who had a total meltdown mentioned earlier and the other is a woman I had never met. She was involved with the cloned super soldier narrative supposedly born out of a test tube. There was no intimacy or predation on either, not having even met with the latter. He is also the one that has several handles and comes into chats, "redpill being one" making these accusations. He actually has been using his wife's phone to make threats to our new producer in scary deep voices without taking her name off the call. It's as if he wants to be caught, maybe a cry for help. What is even worse in emails sent to friends and others in ufology he claims to have receipts from women I have preyed upon? I don't remember handing out receipts let alone preying on anyone? Is it normal to give someone a receipt after imaginary sex? A bill? Is that an Earth custom I missed? Is it standard to say thank you for allowing me to prey upon you, here is a voucher? Where is the logic, why isn't anyone asking in what fantasy land do people give receipts?

He says he has all the goods and had to rescue several women in his delusional savior role but cannot come up anyone other than the two that have been easily dismissed. I have not been intimate with several women over the time he was producing the show so there was no one to rescue other than what was created in his own delusional mind. That is why the term fictitious 8 came about.

Again, anyone who knows me knows it is completely against my nature to do anything aggressive towards women let alone do anything against their will. What is sad is we are going to have to resort to legal action do to defamation of character and stalking. These actions are why he made the list. We know exactly what he is doing, people that know me personally forwarded his messages which has developed into a slam dunk case of stalking and slander.

We also know the real reasons for the false accusations. There was never any personal responsibility on his part only the need for revenge blaming us for his total failure to produce a timely show if at all due to the continuous melt downs. What is sad is people will automatically believe these delusions and judge without ever doing their own research or take into account the character of the one making the accusations. This is epidemic in the UFO community. We are hoping he gets the counseling he needs before his karma catches up to him yet realize some people just need some real hard lessons before they will take personal responsibility.

13. Super Soldiers

There is a lot of literally crazy stuff happening within the super soldier and secret space fleet community. Some are proving not to be who they profess to be. Some are opportunists, some have a very checkered past while others seem to be morally and ethically challenged which is why ECETI has distanced itself from the majority it. Another reason why we do not support the two radio show hosts that put on these conferences. I do however support Corey Goode and a few in the community because he was the first to come out with detailed information about the secret space force, dark fleets, the Nazi connections, twenty and back along with the names of the ships such as Solar Warden and other specific detailed information often parroted by others. Others some of which unfortunately have become his greatest adversaries.

I have my own connections that can and do verify much of what he is saying. These same Whitehat connections with the highest clearances have verified many in the UFO community are connected to the Illuminati, the alphabet agencies and military milabs with hidden agendas. They are what is known as controlled opposition in some cases in others deeply in need of attention. They are not who they profess to be.

I do not question Corey's heart or his motives I do however question the hearts and motives of those around him which have engaged in some very nefarious behavior. Jay Widner and Cliff High launched a major character assassination to discredit me after inviting Corey Goode to speak at Eceti. They were making good on their threats that David Wilcox and Corey Goode would never work again in the spiritual and UFO community. Read David's letter of resignation, especially the part where he denounces attaching himself and his work to the perpetuation of a Luciferian God. Cliff High on Jay's show told people to charge the gates at our conference where Corey Goode was attending as a speaker. He said it is a public event and they have a right to be there even though it was a private event on private property. He also made some beyond ridiculous statements trying to discredit UFO videos which immediately discredited himself exposing his agenda. Thousands of people that have come to ECETI and had their own experience, witnessed and filmed the ships themselves made their voices known. His connections to Tavistock, N.W.O. Inc and utilizing AI computer programs to guide those who follow him is a path I am in total disagreement with. We need to be driven from the heart, the God within, AI will end up being one of the biggest threats to humanity in the future.

I did however notice a woman at their table I once dated years ago. The relationship ended when I was issued an ultimatum to give up ECETI and my work and move to Vegas or the relationship was over. Of course, that was out of the question, Vegas is totally not frequency specific to the work I do and I made it clear that was not on the table. While in Vegas there was a multidimensional war filmed right over the house where I was staying. This refusal opened up a can of worms, black magic, effigies of me being destroyed by her "coven". Sledgehammers taken to effigies of myself where I actually felt the blow. When I realized where it was coming from it lost its effect. Luckily, I have dealt with black magic before. Anyone knowledgeable of the dark arts knows full well it has consequences. Trying to influence or harm another is tabu with any enlightened being. I find it odd the very people practicing dark arts are the ones accusing others of practicing black magic. This was the origin of some of their slanderous remarks.

We all have past lives, karmic cleanups where we have choices to serve the light or the dark, some relationships are reenactments of choices made in the past, again an opportunity to heal yet in some cases the same choices are made that did not end well in the past. This was one of those cases. I would imagine this is what Jay based his accusations on. This was all an attempt to persuade me to stop Corey Goode from speaking at ECETI. Again, anyone that knows me knows I don't respond to threats and they actually inspire me to go in the opposite direction. This backfired on them when I posted the character assassinations, false accusations, lack of character and spiritual advancement on their part as demonstrated by their words and actions. I would also suggest it might be wise to use a little discernment in the company they keep. They threatened to sue me for posting verbatim their slanderous comments bringing everything out in the open for everyone to see. You can't sue someone for cataloging their statements and telling the truth. I didn't even defend the accusations having nothing to hide.

These rumors have consequences. Many started out of jealousy or a self-righteous judgement or projection of what some think is going on generated in their own mind verses what is truly going on. With some people it is hard to believe it is possible to have loving friends of the opposite sex and not be sexually involved. I have been met with some very large angry women at events loaded for bear. One confronted me with all kinds of accusations. I was perplexed because I did not know what she was talking about. She then went to the event coordinator in Detroit and told them I had a line of women going into my room, some underage scantily dressed based on seeing me get into an elevator with two young women. She failed to mention their parents were with them, they were on their way to the swimming pool in the hotel. I asked, "How are you folks doing." That was the extent of my interaction.

Many of the volunteers at the conference were having melt downs at the event due to the pressure of the event and the interference of unseen negative influences. We cleared them and gave them tools to keep themselves clear and heal unseen negative influences. Those were the only people who entered the room. It seems no good deed goes unpunished. This is the nonsense we have to deal with in public along with projections of very nasty energies by those participating in the gossip. Try being sensitive and telepathic with those energies being projected at you. They wonder why they don't have contact. That along with the myriad of unseen negative influences many are packing at these conferences makes it hard to attend. Some have degenerated to the level those who are sensitive can no longer attend. Lately I have chosen to Skype or Zoom any appearances at these events due to all the hidden agendas, chaos and drama that comes with large gatherings. Most of the authentic and enlightened have left the carnival.

14. Divine Feminine Intervention

If it wasn't for Mother Mary's intervention and healing as a child I would not be here. I have always been kind, loving and supportive empowering the divine feminine. The UFO community is not a community as most view communities. It is more like a den filled with agendas, rumors, gossip, jealousy, competition, opportunists, one up man ship behaviors that are often opposite the persona shown on stage.

Something I and many others who are authentic wish no longer to be a part of. I have watched the same thing happen to a host of other people I admire with unquestionable integrity.

Many are leaving or have left the field doing work outside the, "Community," for this very reason. From the top down it has little to do with disclosure and the awakening and healing of humanity and the Earth. There are Luciferians at the top with unlimited funding.

There are those within the Rockefeller initiative. There are government shills, massive egos and morally bankrupt people on the upper levels just like it is in politics. There are event coordinators that choose name recognition over character to sell tickets knowing full well the dubious character of their speakers. There are those who are critical thinking and research impaired that will do the bidding of the upper echelons, become their attack dogs if necessary to rise within the community. There are the opportunists, all one has to do is dangle a little fame and money their way. Sadly, there are those who worship and blindly follow these morally and integrity challenged people lacking all discernment when the obvious is staring them in the face.

Photo by Kan of Mother Mary appearing at ECETI

I apologize to the very few left with impeccable integrity on the moral high ground. In no way do I put them in the same group as the others. There are people of noble character, beautiful Grandmothers, Elders and healers associated with ufology. The good news is they are and will be the contacted by the beautiful many benevolent masters and off worlders. As for the others many are working with low level contacts or malevolent beings some in ignorance, some willingly. There are the morally and ethically challenged icons perpetuating a controlled narrative. Often the most famous in the field. Some are just spiritually challenged dismissing anything other than nuts and bolts and cannot comprehend anything outside their knowingness. They are also blocking contact, part of the controlled narrative. Consider this a warning to any naive authentic people entering the field of Ufology. They will use you, chew you up and spit you out.

15. Spiritual Adeptness

Speaking of spiritual adeptness. No one knows what another soul needs for completion. Byron Katie says there are three kinds of business, your business, other people's business and Gods business. Other people's business is Gods business. Imagine the time and energy wasted with other people's business. Time and energy that could be used to straighten out your own business. Making other people's business your business only establishes one's own ignorance, character, and spiritual evolution.

The things that you judge, condemn and anger you in others is in most cases within yourself. The things you accuse others of often is what you yourself are doing. This is being played out today on a very grand scale. No one knows what another soul needs for completion, what karma is being worked out and what happens between two consenting adults is not others business. Unless one be lie ves it makes their ego superior and there is fame and fortune to be made on the backs of others in their self-righteous acts. Spiritual ego is not spiritual nor is it superior.

Hopefully in time some will gain this understanding and get back on track.

I was speaking to a Hawaiian Grandmother. I have heard the same stories from other Native American Grandmothers. They speak of the old ways. They say they never married in the old days. People came together because they were guided spiritually and separated because it was time, things lasted as long as they were supposed to. There was little or no jealousy, the kids were raised by the tribe, although they had Chiefs and Kings the Grandmothers, the wise ones were in charge. There were no contracts, no divorces or legal battles, no fights over property, no one owned the land or the kids. There was love just not the controls and ownership we call love in today's society.

The concept of owning someone was not in their culture. They worked together for the betterment of the tribe or nation and the Elders were highly respected and taken care of by the younger ones who did the heavy lifting. The victim role was not worshipped and perpetuated as in today's society. Imagine going back to that way of life?

Victims which as stated before often came with agendas and when those agendas were not met then they became the victims followed by persecuting those who did not fill their agendas. The gain they are seeking is often validation, emotional or financial support which the saviors love to provide in an attempt to feel good about themselves. Guess who is labeled the persecutor branded with a myriad of labels when they do not meet the victim's needs? The saviors. The victims not getting what they want persecute the saviors and the merry-go-round goes on and on. Anyone operating on a higher level of consciousness would not engage in all this. The advanced civilizations have transcended war, disease, poverty, fear and insecurity. They are totally free to go where their soul prompts them. A far cry from most civilizations on Earth. Despite our follies these advanced beings are still assisting in the planetary liberation, the awakening and healing of humanity and Earth. It we are going to work with them we need to rise to the occasion.

One big thorn in the ass of those engaging in these character assassinations is why are the Masters, Spiritually and Technologically Advanced beings appearing at ECETI for over 40 years. Why are they appearing to us and not to them? Do they know something the Masters don't? Do they hold themselves superior, wiser?

The second question is why are there so many eyewitnesses in the tens of thousands with pictures, and videos of the ships. Photos of Ascended Masters and advanced off world visitors taken mostly by impartial guests, prominent people from all walks of life. Other paranormal and UFO investigators have acquired evidence one of which is a Taoist monk named Kan who took amazing pictures of the Masters while at ECETI. There is also long list of spontaneous healings from broken wrists, broken backs, tumors, ulcers and a myriad of other afflictions. What kind of person would try to discount or interfere in this and what is guiding them to do so?

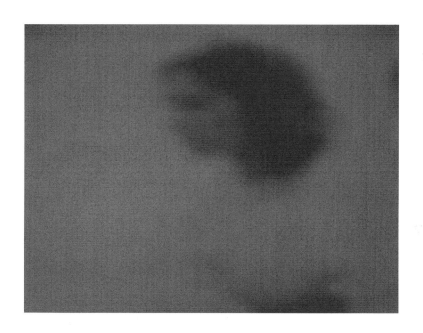

Photo by Kan of Baba Ji at ECETI

Photo by Kan of Cazekiel at ECETI

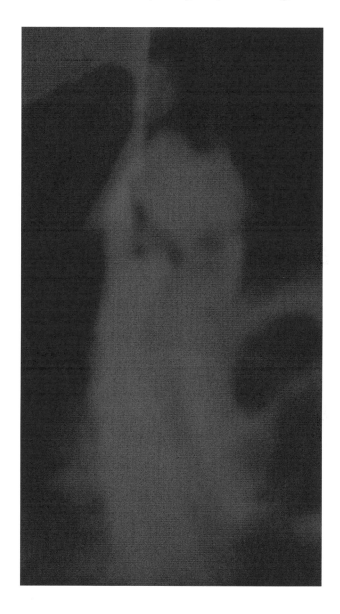

Photo by Kan of Kwan Yin at ECETI

The third question is why are those in control of the UFO community censoring it? One more question is who are these detractors working for, if they are not serving the light, who or what are they serving? Is it their own egos or a much sinister force? What is in it for them. What kind of person would try to take down over 37 years of work, a high vibrational vortex providing healing, support, and education totally dedicated to the awakening and healing of Humanity and the Earth. This is a question they should be asking themselves with brutal honesty. Glad I am not having their light review or the recipient for the karmic boomerang.

Anyone who is authentic, of high moral character and integrity that has contact with evidence to back it up is a threat. I saw a meme that said it best, "They are just angry because the truth you speak contradicts the lie they live." Another meme was, "Your very presence pisses off their demons."

We know who is on the ships, some by name, we know their agendas and their cultures. We know who is behind the awakening, healing and liberation of humanity and the Earth. We know who is trying to suppress it, who wants to keep humanity in the dark, uneducated, sick, poor and enslaved. Why don't they want you to know? The field of ufology has to clean up its act unless they want to continue to serve a darker agenda on the downward spiral. The benevolent beings are waiting. How many knives can you pull out of your back, how many betrayals, how many unfounded rumors gossip and slander must one endure before they say enough. I believe for me that question has been answered.

Again I struggled with releasing this information. If just one of them apologized and redirected their energies you would never hear about them. The reason I am putting out this information is to warn people things are not what they seem in the UFO community just as in politics or any other institution. It is also an attempt to dispel some of the slander, gossip and unfounded accusations and rumors. Most spawned from jealousy, competition, projections, and the classic accuse others of what you yourself are doing. There are also some very unstable people in the community. Let's not forget the influence of unseen negative influences and the posers threatened by the authentic. Just as Mother Mary said,

"Universal Peace shall not come through governments and religions but through the hearts and minds of the people."

It is the same with contact. It will come through the hearts and minds of the people. Those with an open mind, loving heart and pure intent. Farmers, gardeners, carpenters, plumbers, electricians, children, those who are in service to others, those who spend time in nature that are grounded in the basics, are humble and of good character, they are the ones being contacted.

There needs to be new venues. In these venues there has to be vetting, a weeding out of the posers, those who are not authentic and those who are in it for fame, fortune, or other hidden agendas. A higher frequency needs to be held at these events if the higher frequency beings seen and unseen are to attend. That is my solution to fixing this problem. Some things are not fixable, there will be too much resistance and too much money involved to change. They will take the downward spiral. Best to start over with something new.

In the past I have been very supportive of the UFO community. Now I recommend people to avoid it altogether other than a small handful of people.

When I look back at what I have written in this chapter maybe that was the goal, to save others from what I went through or at least open their eyes so they are not blind sided when they go to these events. If you are looking for contact with spiritually and technologically advance beings my advice is to go out into nature. Fill your heart with love, joy and bliss. Send it out to them. Do everything to raise your own frequency and make your own personal connection with God/Creator/Great Spirit. Ground yourself. The more grounded you are the more spiritual energies you can bring in. It is an internal process not and external process. No one can do it for you. It is your quest, some can support you in that quest but only if they empower you to reach your highest potential and not leave you in dependency or worship. The see me, dig me worship me days are over. A hard lesson is coming, a well earned one I might add for those who have taken that path.

There are always lessons to be learned, wisdom to gain from these experiences, rather than succumb to them we can turn sour grapes into wine. I realized my message would be censored by conference organizers, radio and TV networks, even book publishers took the money from sales, filed bankruptcy and used the money for their own personal gain. There would always be people for various reasons that would block the message and I would have no control. I decided the only way these messages could get out was if I built my own conference building, created my own radio and television shows and published my own books. That is how the 70 acre ranch, an internationally known UFO hotspot and spiritual vortex as well as ECETI Stargate Radio, As You Wish Talk Radio with BBS and ECETI Stargate TV came into being. When the universe rolls boulders your way build stairs.

Now take a deep breath, release any energies while connecting to these people and events, drop into the heart and focus on love joy and bliss. Again the main reason I wrote this chapter is to save a lot of time and energy by avoiding these pitfalls, to help people avoid giving their power away to those undeserving, those not empowering you as an individual and move on with your own personal contact with God/Creator/Great Spirit and the beautiful many you will meet along the way.

Bless you if you have made it this far, the tell all is over. I struggled with removing this altogether, yet it needs to be said not just for my own release but to bring clarity as to the controlled narrative, controlled opposition, posers, shills along with the integrity and morally challenged in the industry. Yes, a multibillion dollar industry. One has to transcend all this or avoid it altogether to make contact with Spiritually and Technologically Advanced beings. You have everything you need within you.

Onward and Upward Who is Who in the Multiverse.

The Universe is filled with life beyond human comprehension. There are over one billion trillion planets out there that can sustain life according to scientists. This is only the third dimension. Scientists agree there are at least 11 dimensions yet in truth the multiverse is infinitely large and infinitely small. The numbers increase as technology expands further into the great unknown. There comes a time when scientists will eventually have to abandon their technology to truly understand the multiverse we live in. The world of consciousness and energy. Einstein said, "Alas I am without all mathematics to touch upon forever." This is a big step for most scientists which cling to the recycled ignorance taught in most curriculum. Some may feel this is a harsh statement yet imagine the harsh statements and actions made to anyone who thinks outside the box. They often say you cannot prove any of this. They demand you measure nonphysical events with physical instruments yet where is the logic? There are highly sensitive instruments that can now prove there are unseen influences at play, yet it is still defined by the observers beliefs.

"Scientists are often prisoners in their own test tubes."

We are multidimensional beings existing on a vibration continuum, limiting yourself to a body and a personality limits your awareness of the multidimensional world in which we live. These next understandings are beyond the physical and personality self yet can influence and impact both. Which leads us into who is who in the multiverse. Despite the insanity we will continue to educate and empower the individual. these next chapters will bring a greater understanding to ufology without censorship, the spiritual ultradimensional aspect and true history.

16. The Vibrational Continuum and the Electromagnetic Light Spectrum

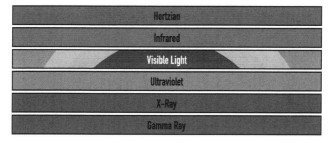

CONSCIOUSNESS EXPRESSED THROUGH THE ELECTROMAGNETIC SPECTRUM

| Hertzian |
| Infrared |
| Visible Light |
| Ultraviolet |
| X-Ray |
| Gamma Ray |

We can only see a fraction of 0.005% of the electromagnetic spectrum which is visible light

जया

The electro magnetic light spectrum and how it ties into dimensions or levels of consciousness.

The infrared is also known as the astral level or 4d. It is the first visible unseen realm to those who are becoming clairvoyant. It is a very vast dimension. On the lowest levels are astral beings, disturbed and degenerate humans that have crossed over and did not go to the light, demoniacs, greys, reptilians, royal reptilians, serpent beings, Jinn there is what is referred to as the Orion Alliance a consortium of greys, reptilians and other malevolent self-serving beings. This is not to be confused with the Orion Council of Light which are planetary liberators from the 6th dimension. There are Tulkas conjured beings sent to do harm and poltergeists, usually children that are stuck in the 4th that need healing. The House of Mary is good to get them the help they need. This is the foundation for many scary movies that when you know who you are and have the tools to set boundaries and heal unseen negative influences they are not scary at all.

The lower 4th and the degenerate beings existing that are in the process of being healed or removed altogether. Unfortunately as the veils between worlds become thinner there are bleed throughs and influences into the 3rd. We can often have excessive anger, sadness, deviant influences coming from this level. We must keep a constant vigil on our thoughts and feelings so as not to be affected. We have a saying if you don't like what you are feeling do a healing. These influences can come through friends, lovers and family hijacking one's ascension process and soul evolution. Many in ignorance or willingly are allowing these influences to work through them for personal gain, fame, money, and power. Some are just trying to fill a void, the love and acceptance they did not get as a child. The come from and motive within each individual needs to be monitored constantly with brutal honesty if one is to stay on the path of enlightenment. How to heal these unseen negative influences will be addressed later.

The mid levels in the 4d or astral level are filled with everyday people, animals etc. waiting for their next incarnation. Many loved ones contact us from that level if they did not get past the psychic barrier between the 4th and 5th dimension. The higher levels in the 4th have guides and teachers that can be beneficial yet there is some degree of division, attachment to culture, religion, any separative belief that keeps them from ascending into the 5th dimension past the psychic barrier. Some have less dense physical bodies, some energy bodies and their worlds are just a physical to them as ours matching their frequency. The 5th dimension is where one knows themselves to be Creator and Creator knows itself to be human which comes in many sizes, shapes and colors. It is Unity Consciousness. Beings operating in the 5th adhere to Universal Law. They can drop into the 4th and 3rd to assist, inspire and protect in most cases. The Pleiadeans are mostly in the 5th, some are helping in the 3rd and 4th others have ascended to the 7th. They are very active in the planetary liberation of Humanity and the Earth.

We work a lot with many known masters throughout the dimensions, Jesus, Quan Yin, the House of Mary, Baba ji, White Eagle, Buffalo Calf Woman, Cazekiel, an ascended version of Ezekiel, Blaji a 7d Pleiadean, Plemaria 5d, Nia 5d, Coeea 5d Pleiadean and a warrior named Ciavon which is new, here now with the gloves off. He and his group come from a warrior planet much like the Jedi starwars characters. We are also working with Bagit 5d Sirian feline, Bacal and Eha 7d lion being felines in ancient times known as the protectors of the Gods and a host of Ascended Masters, others too numerous to mention including Inner Earth beings.

The 6th dimension is where beings identify more with God/Creator/Great Spirit. Personal identity is no longer important. It is only used for reference points in communication. The Orion Council of Light is in the 6th dimension but they to are helping in the 4th and 3rd. They are planetary liberators having gone through the Orion Wars coming out victorious. Arcturians are also in the 6th. They are behind many of the crop circles. They play more of a spiritual advisory role.

Many have merged with what some call their soul mate and come as both male and female. Others have made God/Creator/Great Spirit their soul mate. Cazekiel is a classic example of this. Ezekiel of old merged with Cassia and ascended into the 7th dimension. In these dimensions many mergers occur. Baba Jesus where Baba ji the Yogi Christ and Jesus merge as a blend of East and West is a beautiful example of this. They have transcended all religious and cultural divisions in the 6th and 7th and these levels are best known as levels of consciousness rather than levels of identity. You have the House of Mary where Mother Mary, Mary Magdalene, the Grandmothers hold the divine feminine energy. Quan Yin the Goddess of wrathful compassion has made several visitatons to the Ranch with several photographs of her manifesting from a light body to an almost physical body. The Shakina energies encompass all the divine feminine beings throughout all the cultures on and off world. Many other houses of consciousness holding other frequencies. Love, Wisdom, Healing, Protection many houses attract beings who are masters in these fields. The House of Michael and the House of Rama are good examples of protection, the Lion Beings protectors of the Gods, the Humanoid felines from Sirius and Lyra are also top of the line when it comes to protection. There are no limits to the forms Creators protection can take. Many of the ancient ones represent what is within ourselves and act as reminders or place holders. They are not to be worshipped they are to be respected and honored. There is a danger in worshiping external beings, you give your power away and become what many refer to as a leaky battery. Always remember God/Creator/Great Spirit is within, as Buddha said the whole Universe is within you. They are helpers along the way to your becoming the Master, making your own personal God/Creator/Great Spirit connection. Always remember the name of God is coded into your DNA, YOD HE VAV HE, "YA-WEH" you have the genes of the Gods time to activate them.

The 7th dimension is total atonement or at-one-ment. It is where entities are totally emersed in God/Creator/Great Spirit. It is possible to walk the Earth while totally aligned with the 7th. This is exemplified by Jesus saying, "I of myself do nothing, it is the father through me doing the work." This is where the personality self or ego comes into total alignment with the God within. It is where one becomes a vessel of God/Creator/Great Spirit. This is the end goal of enlightenment. Ascension. Concerning ascension many are going about it backwards. It is not desiring to leave this wretched planet, it is mastering judgement, emotions, seeing the God in everyone and everything and grounding it fully in the body. This creates the quickening, the rise in frequency in every atom, cell, muscle, tissue and fiber of your being. Then you take the body with you.

After the 7th dimension is the void, after that is the 8th, 9th, 10th, up to the 13th dimension. Realms beyond the imagination of most. Some of which are coming here during the planetary awakening and healing of humanity and the Earth. We have experienced collectives from the 8th to 13th dimension. The Jasai planetary protectors, the

Laka 13th dimensional beings assisting and a host of others.

Here is a chart to help you understand who is who in the multiverse. It is limited and flexible, can be added to as more contacts occur.

13TH DIMENSIONAL BEYOND THE VOID - JASAI WORLD PROTECTORS OF THE WORLD
11TH DIMENSIONAL BEYOND THE ELOHIM – ASCENSION COLLECTIVE KNOWN AS LKA
7TH DIMENSIONAL PLEIADIANS/SIRIANS – LION BEINGS/ORIONS/GOD-GODDESS BEINGS/PLANE OF ETERNAL BLISS/ANDROMEDANS/BENEVOLENT ANUNNAKI ETC
6TH DIMENSIONAL PLEIADIANS/SIRIANS-PANTHERS/ORIONS/INNER EARTH/ETC
5TH DIMENSIONAL AUCTURIANS/PLEIADIANS/SIRIANS-FELINE/INNER EARTH/CHRIST CONS
4TH DIMENSIONAL ELEMENTALS/PLEIADIANS/ORIONS, SOME ASCENDED MASTERS/ALCYONS
NEUTRAL BEINGS - WATCHERS
NEUTRAL GREYS
3RD DIMENSIONAL HUMANITY HOST OF OTHER BEINGS THROUGOUT THE GALAXY
LIMITING THOUGHT FORMS/WOUNDED COLLECTIVE CONSCIOUSNESS
ARCHONS/ILLUMINATTI/WOUNDED HUMANITY
DISCARNATE SOULS
TALL GREYS - MALEVOLENT
REPTILLIANS
SERPENT BEINGS
HYBRIDS – GREY/REPTILLIAN NASTIES
FALLEN ANUNNAKI

This is a chart the represents the multidimensional bodies of the human experience. We have a body within a body all the way back to source. As one ascends up the vibrational continuum one meets other beings that correspond with the frequency of that body. Buddha said the whole universe resides within you. When you reach 7d you are one with the one consciousness that encompasses all consciousness on all planes and dimensions. It is no longer them it is all you. The spark has become the full flame.

CHAKRAS AND ENERGY BODIES

Cosmic Body
I AM Body
Spiritual Body
Etheric Body
Astral Body
Emotional Body
Mental Body
Physical Body

Crown Chakra
Third Eye Chakra
Throat Chakra
Heart Chakra
Solar Plexus Chakra
Sacral Chakra
Root Chakra

जया

Different civilizations exist within the vibrational continuum.

On the journey to self-realization and self-mastery it is imperative to maintain a strong moral compass, balance, and be forever vigilant to maintain humility so as not to fall into spiritual ego or fall under the influence of seen and unseen negative influences. It is also imperative that we stay in service to others, clear our own wounds, traumas, and wrong conclusions from past experiences. These unhealed patterns are chinks in our spiritual armor that allow unseen negative influences to hijack our mission and soul purpose. We need to remain flexible in our truth because truth has many levels, truth often changes with new information, truth also does not need defending and stands on its own merit. In India they have a saying the closer you get to Nirvana the more the demons rear their ugly heads. The greater your light the more the moths come to the flame as well as unseen negative influences. It is imperative we learn to be vigilant in clearing ourselves others and our surroundings. It is helpful to remember, as we ascend, we become a mirror and amplifier of everything others love and don't love about themselves. The higher frequencies accelerate the healing process of those around us. We cannot shrink with fear or sadness when others project and criticize us nor swell with pride when they praise us. Best to remain neutral and centered in your own personal God/Creator/Great Spirit connection.

Another understanding in self-mastery is no one will ever see or know you for who you are they can only see from their own reference points and projections. Only the ego needs defending. When you are challenged clear any unseen negative influences and practice loving detachment. Humor also plays an important role which is why you see Yogis and Lamas often laughing at the follies of man/woman as well as themselves mastering judgement of self and others. They understand the true nature of the, all loving and all forgiving omnipresent God, The Creator within all Creation. They also understand no one knows what another soul needs for completion. The last thing we want to impart is to be authentic. Everyone has their own unique purpose. When you are authentic you are standing in your power. These understandings are first and foremost in Self-Mastery. We recommend you read this imparted knowledge throughout your path to enlightenment as a reminder to help depersonalize the many challenges along the way.

Healing Unseen negative influences

Healing is a must for all those who desire to operate in other realms of consciousness. You must maintain self- authority and control. If you are experiencing negative vibrations, they are either thought forms, limiting mental concepts, psychic bonds, discarnate entities (lost souls) in need of healing or unseen entities from other dimensions. Discarnate entities or (lost souls) are bound to the earth vibration due to lower vibrational attitudes and emotions. Some are coercive and desire to manipulate and control. Love heals. It is the ultimate power in the Universe. Casting out only sends them to another place, another person. In all healing, remember that God is love. It is the power of love that heals and releases.

STEPS TO CLEAR THE ENERGY

1. Close your aura by visualizing a white or gold light around you.

2. Call upon God/Creator/Great Spirit , the Father/Mother God or your chosen cultural representative of God, be it Jesus, Buddha, Babaji, Mary, Mohammed, White Eagle or another one of the Beautiful Many Christed Ones.

3. Tell the entities they are healed and forgiven, lifted and enlightened.

4. Tell them they are healed and surrounded with the Christ light and the Christ love. You can use the light and love of your chosen representative as long as they have ascended. .

5. Ask your chosen representative to take them to their perfect place.

6. Ask that all negative thought forms and limiting mental concepts be dissolved and lifted in the light of truth.

7. Ask that all psychic bonds be severed, and the

auras of all to be closed to all but spirit of the highest vibration.

Repeat this process until you feel clear. There may be more than one healing to do. Remember your word is very powerful, and what is spoken on their level manifests instantly. They ARE filled and surrounded with light. Many enlightened ones use this process before opening to spirit or any spiritual practice.

It creates a clear and safe environment, and it also lifts the one who is doing the healing. Intent is nine-tenths of the law. If you intend to serve and heal, you will draw to you entities of like mind. If you intend to coerce or manipulate, again you will draw entities of like mind. It is the law of attraction.

At times, discarnate spirits will come to your light like a moth to a flame. Do not judge yourself, simply heal them. They are the ones in trouble, not you. They are seeking your help.

SHORT FORM OF CLEARING PRAYER

AFTER DOING THE ABOVE IN THE
BEGINNING   (FIRST CALL IN YOUR MAIN TEACHER
OR GUIDE AND OTHER DIVINE BEINGS CHRISTED
OR ABOVE) THEN SAY

*"WE WELCOME ALL ENTITIES IN LOVE AND LIGHT
WE SPEAK TO YOU FROM THE LORD GOD OF OUR
BEING TELLING YOU ALL YOU ARE HEALED AND
FORGIVEN LIFTED AND ENLIGHTENED FILLED AND
SURROUNDED BY THE CHRIST LIGHT AND THE
CHRIST LOVE AND WE ASK THE BEAUTIFUL MANY
TO ESCORT YOU OFF TO YOUR PERFECT PLACE GO
IN PEACE"*

17. Yi Gong, Yoga, Manifesting Ceremonies, World and Personal Healing Meditations

Yi Gong is a very ancient practice traced back from India, China, Tibet, Egypt and some say Atlantis and Lemuria. Some of the most ancient statues show masters holding mudras and poses practicing Yi Gong. The bases of Yi Gong is less is more. The simpler the form the more powerful. It is a practice where one masters the elements, merges with them opening up energy channels that bring healing, peace and well being in our everyday lives. It begins with tapping the body from toes to head to energize and bring chi into the body, then the Earth, Fire, Water and Air movements followed by a meditation posture that opens the energy channels of the body. The practice is part of the Self Mastery Ambassador training.

Yoga has many forms the word stands for All Encompassing. The form of Yoga we recommend is Bhakti Yoga which addresses the Spirit, Mind and Body. Each posture brings consciousness to different areas of the body allowing healing and more flexibility. The feet and legs represent our understanding. Hips flexibility. Lower back represents support either emotional or financial. Stomach represents being able to digest information and concepts. The heart is all about love, a constricted heart or the inability to love can result in heart attacks. Hands and arms the ability to grasp, shoulders are all about carrying sometimes people or situations we need to let go. Neck also represents flexibility, people who need to control often have neck problems. The head represents your beliefs in the world. There is always a lie in be lie f and we have to be flexible in our be lie fs. Being in the head and not in the heart can create overuse, headaches, migraines in worse case scenarios tumors.

Yoga can bring relief, healing and flexibility to each of these areas yet all aspects, Spirit Mind and Body need to be addressed for balance. The mind is a wonderful servant but a terrible master. The heart is connected to the soul and that should be our source of guidance. The intellect is a drop in the sea of consciousness. Yoga workshops are held regularly at ECETI.

18. Manifesting Ceremony

There are many forms of manifesting. The best form is to be in alignment with your own unique soul purpose. Then things flow like a river. For this to happen we need to release the past, heal any wounds, traumas and wrong conclusions from past experiences. These block the flow.

There is a ceremony yogis use that has several steps.

1. Clear using the healing prayer and create sacred space.
2. Meditate on what you desire, keep it down to three things and make it personal.
3. Write it down on a piece of paper.
4. Say it out loud, if you cannot say it out loud there is a block. If you feel embarrassed or unworthy sit with it. Go within and ask why. Healing and releasing the block is a gift in itself. Get an abalone shell and put some sage in it. Ignite it and wave the smoke over you

with each desired manifestation spoken aloud.

5. Burn the paper and release it to the Universe. Do it in a safe way such as fire pit or metal container with proper ventilation.

R.U.C.A.T. Treatment

This form of manifestation comes from the T.I.C. Teachings of the Inner Christ.

It is a form of meditation that aligns one with source. God/Creator/Great Spirit. Each letter represents a statement to assist in the manifestation process.

R. Recognize God/Creator/Great Spirit as Omnipresent, "Everywhere Present". Omnipotent, "All Powerful". Omnicient, "All Knowing", Omniscient, all sensing. The source of infinite possibilities.

U. Unify. Become one with God/Creator/Great Spirit knowing there are no divisions in

Omnipresence. Feel the love joy and bliss of Creator.

C. Claim the desired manifestation what ever you want to experience or manifest yet a caution always ask in the highest and best good for all when dealing with another person it is against universal law to trespass on the free will of another.

A. Accept the manifestation in the present moment, see it as if it already happened, visualize it and embrace it. In doing so you collapse time and bring it into your present world. In some cases it takes a little time for the universe to rearrange itself to bring to you the desired manifestation.

T. Thanks. Giving thanks and an attitude of gratitude is one of the quickest ways of manifesting. Giving thanks as if it has already manifested again brings the desired manifestation into the present moment.

Focusing on the desired manifestation, visualize it imagine yourself living the desired outcome and energizing it with love, joy and bliss greatly assists the desired outcome.

19. World and Personal Healing Meditation

Cazekiels Wheel World and Personal Healing meditation. The meditation video is available at www.eceti.org. We will walk those through who want to do it by themselves or in groups. Always begin by healing any unseen negative energies thus creating sacred space.

1. Visualize a crystalline tube of protection around the group only good can enter.

2. Visualize a golden white ball of energy in the center of the group or in the heart for personal meditations.

3. See the ball spinning faster and faster expanding encompassing your entire body or group.

4. As the ball spins faster see it permeating your physical body, every atom, cell, muscle, tissue, bone within your body. You can direct it to places in need or add different colored light to areas in

need. Violet for transmutation, blue and green for healing, orange for energy etc.

5. Visualize the energy flowing through your mental body and emotional body cleansing any thought forms, wrong conclusions from past experience, fears, doubts, self judgements, and judgements of others.

6. Visualize the light healing all past life traumas, allow the wisdom to settle into the soul, bring in the light of forgiveness to thoroughly cleanse your astral body.

7. Feel yourself expanding into your etheric body, your perfect incarnation, your whole and healthy perfect self. Allow your etheric body to communicate and recode your DNA.

8. As the ball of light is expanding spinning faster and faster feel yourself expanding into the 5th dimension, into unity consciousness, Christ or Buddha consciousness. Expand in awareness filling yourself with love, joy, bliss and healing energies as far as you can go. Expand into the I AM, The Godself, the Cosmic Self.

9. Now that you are fully emersed from that position send energy back down all the lower bodies and into the Earth. Visualize it moving out

in all 4 directions, the North, South, East and West until the entire planet is surrounded with the awakening and healing light of God/Creator/Great Spirit. You can focus on and send the awakening and healing energy to countries in need or just blanket the Earth.

10. After the meditation is complete feel yourself descending back through the lower bodies coming back to the physical grounding yourself back on Earth and give thanks to the beautiful many Masters, Saints and Sages who participated in the meditation.

Note it is important to close your aura to all but your own Christ, I AM, or Godself, if possible, take your shoes off or sit on the ground. Grounding is essential. The more grounded you are the more consciousness and energy you can bring in and anchor in this world.

20. Sacred Gardening

There are many ways of gardening the more organic and awareness of the land, its energies and working with nature is the best and brings the best yield. Always sit with the land, ask the land for permission as to the location, size and shape of your garden. As a caution if you do not ask permission or put your garden in the wrong place disrespecting the land and spirits of the land there can be consequences. I experienced a very angry Gnome due to disrespect of the previous owner who seemed to enjoy cutting down the trees and leaving trash everywhere.

I had to make peace with him to end his shenanigans. They can make everything go wrong. It is better to seek the benefits of working with them. A place to meditate at the center of your garden to connect with the land and nature spirits asking for their guidance and help is also very beneficial. Sacred geometry, asking which plant goes in which row is also helpful. There are divination techniques that can help guide you in planting. Each plant has a vibration and a quality, when you get it right it creates a harmonic chord and the qualities of one plant support another. Organic materials, fertilizer, such as steer, chicken any barnyard manure the more the better will keep the plants vibrant and healthy. Minerals of rock dust creates disease, insect and frost protection. There are other safe effective organic weed and insect remediation methods we recommend the following books to assist in organic gardening. Don't worry about making mistakes, that is how you learn.

21. Inner Earth

There are many ancient stories about Inner Earth, Shambala, Agartha, advanced civilizations living on the interior. What most people do not know is most advanced civilizations live on the interior of planets. It is much safer from asteroid impacts, Solar events, aggressive ETs and the ravages of nature. All planets are hollow despite many flat earth theories. They are born from Suns as hot gaseous balls of energy that find cradle orbits and over billions of years begin to cool. Due to centripetal force the heavier elements move to the surface, cool and begin to solidify.

The forming planet also gathers material from space along with water from icy comets. There is a sequence of planets in orbit around suns throughout the galaxy. This does not include artificial planets most of which are hollow as well. Your Moon is hollow, it is a terraforming base placed in the perfect orbit to create the tides and other energies necessary to maintain life. Without it everything would be stagnant. In ancient history there are stories of no moon, two moons, then back to one moon. The sun also rose in the west and the stars stood still then shifted representing pole shifts. Everything that ever lived on the surface is preserved on the interior. Yes, even many mythological creatures, including Gnomes, Elven beings and Fairies. There are the remnants of Atlantis and Lemuria that ventured inward to escape the great floods and land upheavels. There are other races some very ancient and less dense physical. This will all unfold in your very near future when granted access. Many of the severe quakes have opened up tunnels with access to the interior.

A word of caution, don't go unless your spiritual house is in order, no hidden agendas. When I said everything is preserved this includes the dinosaurs, they control them with their minds. Not being successful in this could end up in being lunch. One of the great doors is in the Bermuda Triangle which answers the age old question, what happened to the missing planes and ships? Most are in the interior not wanting to go back to the surface. Who would believe them and what would happen to them if they told their story. Admiral Byrd did not fair well.

22. In Summary

In summary everything shared in this book was done in the highest of intention with the purpose of advancing humanity and aiding in the awakening, healing, ascension and planetary liberation of Earth. We have had contact for thousands of years, we along with other nations have been back engineering ships since the 30's. We have used the ancient wisdom of the past, advanced ancient ancestors with their mercury driven Vimanas.

America with its secret space fleet has been going back and forth to the moon and mars in minutes since the 60's. We have massive ships, space stations and colonies throughout the galaxy. We have had anti/counter gravity, fueless energy, miracle healing technologies that have been suppressed by the war and disease profiteers for decades. We have had contact with spiritually and technologically advanced off worlders since the beginning of recorded time. It is time to end the controlled narrative, the division and competition. Stop the withholding of these technologies and take the quantum leap in evolution which has been available to us for quite some time. It is time to end the tyranny. Do with the information as you wish.

About the Author

James Gilliland is a best-selling author, internationally known lecturer, minister, counselor, multiple Near Death Experiencer and contactee. James is recognized world-wide as the founder of the Gilliland Estate, previously referred to and commonly known as the ECETI Ranch (Enlightened Contact with ExtraTerrestrial Intelligence) where he documents and shares amazing multi-dimensional contact phenomenon which can be viewed at www.eceti.org. His weekly As You Wish Talk Radio program on BBSradio.com draws an audience from around the world who are interested in truth and Higher Consciousness.

James's books Reunion with Source, Becoming Gods, and The Ultimate Soul Journey educate, awaken, inform and heal. His latest book – Annunaki Return Star Nations and the Days to Come is a powerful look at what is happening on a multi-dimensional level as we move forward in this time of great change.

He is the host of the documentaries Contact Has Begun & Contact Has Begun 2, and has been featured in documentaries and television shows such as His Story, The History Channel, UFOs then and Now, UFO Hotspots, ABC, Fox News, BBC Danny Dyer Special, Paranormal State, The Uncontrolled Narrative and Disclosure with James Gilliland.

He has also appeared on numerous radio shows including Coast to Coast and Jeff Rense. His unique focus on dispelling the myths propogated by the disinformation system make him an in-demand speaker at events such as the International UFO Congress, Contact in the Desert and the Star Knowledge Conferences. He also hosts ECETI's popular Science, Spirit and World Transformation Conference every summer at the Gilliland Estate.

He is a facilitator of many Eastern disciplines; a visionary dedicated to the awakening and healing of Humanity and the Earth and he teaches higher dimensional realities from experience.

An unprecedented event is unfolding at the Gilliland Ranch near Mt Adams, and Trout Lake, Washington that has the potential to change the course and destiny of Humanity and the Earth. The people of Earth are being offered a chance to join the rest of the universe in peace and participate in spiritual awakening and benevolent Extraterrestrial contact. UFO sightings, Orb phenomena, CE5 Contact & "UFO contact" with spiritually and technologically advanced extra and ultra-terrestrial off world visitors – a "greater family of man" – has occurred at the Gilliland ranch near Mt. Adams.

Website: eceti.org

Printed in Great Britain
by Amazon

40664323R00085